in TAB

Nutcracker *for* Guitar

Table of Contents

Cover art: Shawn McKelvey

Signs and Symbols Used in This Book

⑥ = D — Tune the 6th string down to D.

BIV — Barre the fourth fret. The B indicates a barre across a fret with the first finger. Roman numerals indicate the fret numbers: I = 1, II = 2, III = 3, IV = 4, V = 5, VI = 6, VII = 7, VIII = 8, IX = 9, X =10, XI =11, XII =12.

½ BIV — Barre the fourth fret across three strings.

Pos. — Position

𝄆 𝄇 — Repeat signs

First and second endings:
Play the first ending the first time, play the second ending the second time, skipping the first.

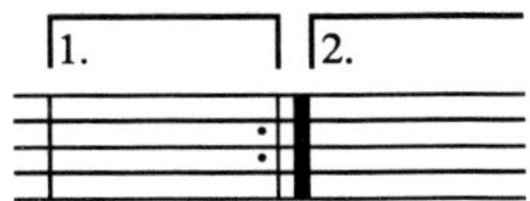

D.S. al Fine — Go back to the sign (𝄋) and end at the Fine.

D.S. al Coda — Go back to the sign (𝄋) and play to the coda sign (𝄌), then skip to the Coda to end the piece.

𝄐 — Fermata: Hold the note longer than its normal value.

Har. 12 — Harmonic at the 12th fret.

〰〰 — Trill

Left Hand Indications:
0 = Open string **1** = First finger **2** = Second finger
3 = Third finger **4** = Fourth finger

Tablature Explanation
Tablature is a system of notation that graphically represents the strings and frets of the guitar fingerboard. Each note is indicated by placing a number, which indicates the fret or finger position to be picked, on the appropriate string. For example:

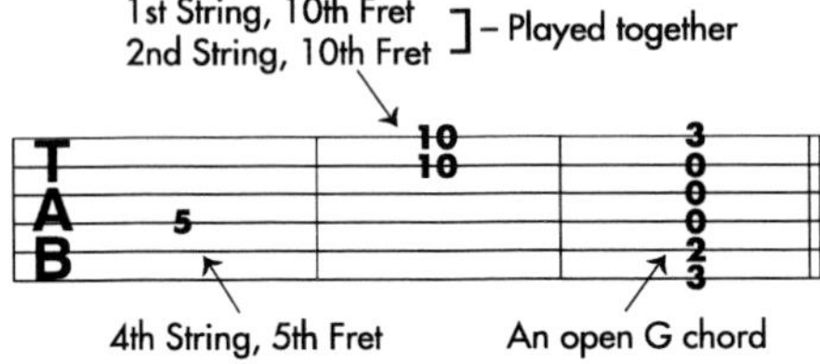

Zeichen und Symbole, die in diesem Buch benutzt werden

⑥ = D — Stimme die 6. Saite auf D herunter.

BIV — Barrée im 4. Bund. Das B bezeichnet einen Barréegriff mit dem 1. Finger (Zeigefinger) über einen Bund. Die römischen Ziffern bezeichnen den jeweiligen Bund. I = 1, II = 2, III = 3, IV = 4, V = 5, VI = 6, VII = 7, VIII = 8, IX = 9, X =10, XI =11, XII =12.

½ BIV — Ein halber Barréegriff (über 3 Saiten) im 4. Bund.

Pos. — Position

𝄆 𝄇 — Wiederholungszeichen

1. und 2. Schluß:
Beim ersten Durchgang spielst Du bis zum 1. Schluß, beim 2. Durchgang überspringst Du den 1. und endest mit dem 2. Schluß.

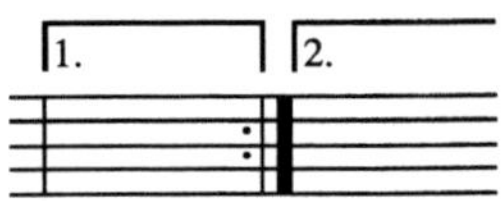

D.S. al Fine — Zurück zu (𝄋) und dann bis zum Schluß.

D.S. al Coda — Zurück zu (𝄋) und von dort bis zur Coda (𝄌), danach die Coda überspringen und bis zum Schluß spielen.

𝄐 — Fermate: Diese Note wird etwas länger gehalten, als es ihrem normalem Notenwert entspricht.

Har. 12 — Flageolett im 12. Bund.

〰〰 — Triller

Fingerbezeichnungen für die linke Hand:
0 - offen gespielte Saite **1** - 1. Finger (Zeigefinger)
2 - 2. Finger (Mittelfinger) **3** - 3. Finger (Ringfinger)
4 - 4. Finger (kleiner Finger)

Erklärung der Tabulatur
Die Tabulatur ist ein Notationssystem für Gitarre, das Saiten und Bünde des Gitarrengriffbretts grafisch darstellt. Die Position der Zahlen gibt den jeweiligen Ton und den jeweiligen Bund an. Zum Beispiel:

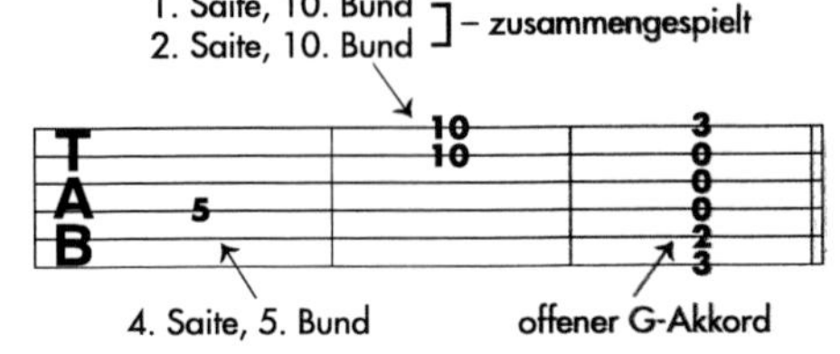

Señales y Simbolos Usados en Este Libro

⑥ = D — Afine la sexta cuerda en Re.

BIV — Haga cejillo en el cuarto traste (espacio). "B" indica un cejillo sobre un traste (espacio) con el primer dedo. Los números romanos indican los números de trastes o espacios: I =1, II = 2, III = 3, IV = 4, V = 5, VI = 6, VII = 7, VIII = 8, IX = 9, X =10, XI =11, XII =12.

½ BIV — Haga cejillo en el cuarto traste (espacio) sobre tres cuerdas.

Pos. — Posición

‖: :‖ — Signo (barra) de repetición

Primeros y segundos finales:
Toque el primer final la primera vez, toque el segundo final la segunda vez, saltándose el primero.

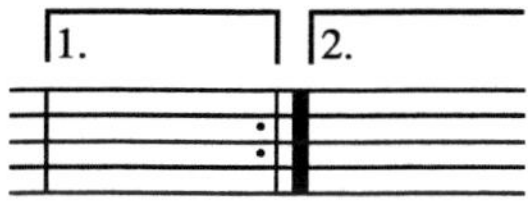

D.S. al Fine — Regrese al signo (𝄋) y termine en Fine.

D.S. al Coda — Regrese al signo (𝄋) y toque hasta el signo de coda (𝄌), luego sáltese a la Coda para terminar la pieza.

𝄐 — Calderón. Sostenga la nota más tiempo de su valor normal.

Har. 12 — Armónico en el duodécimo traste (espacio 12).

~~~~~~~~ — Trino

Indicaciones para la Mano Izquierda:
0 = Cuerda abierta o al aire **1** = Primer dedo
2 = Segundo dedo **3** = Tercer dedo **4** = Cuarto dedo

Explicación de la Tablatura
La Tablatura es un sistema de notación que representa gráficamente las cuerdas y los trastes (espacios) del diapasón. Cada nota se indica poniendo un número, el cual indica el traste o la posición del dedo en la cuerda correspondiente. Por ejemplo:

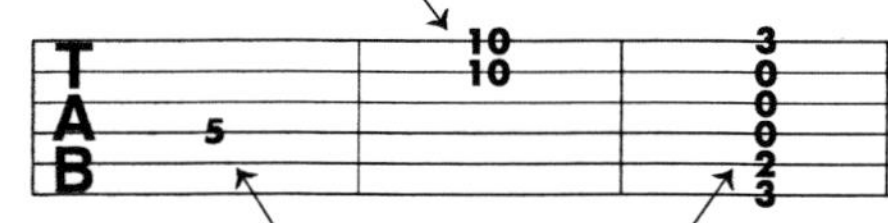

Signes et symboles utilisés dans ce livre

⑥ = D — Accorder la sixième corde en ré.

BIV — Barrer la quatrième frette. Le B indique une barre sur une frette avec le premier doigt. Les chiffres romains indiquent les chiffres de frette. I = 1, II = 2, III = 3, IV = 4, V = 5, VI = 6, VII = 7, VIII = 8, IX = 9, X =10, XI =11, XII =12.

½ BIV — Barrer la quatrième frette sur trois cordes.

Pos. — Position

‖: :‖ — Répéter le signes

Première et deuxième fin:
Jouer la première fin la première fois, jouer la deuxième fin la deuxième fois, en sautant la première.

D.S. al Fine — Retourner au signe (𝄋) et terminer à la Fine.

D.S. al Coda — Retourner au signe (𝄋) et jouer jusqu'au signe du Coda (𝄌), puis sauter le reste jusqu'au Coda pour terminer le morceau.

𝄐 — Fermata. Tenir la note plus longtemps que sa valeur normale.

Har. 12 — Harmonique à la deuxième frette.

~~~~~~~~ — Trille

Indications pour la main gauche:
0 = Corde ouverte **1** = Premier doigt **2** = Second doigt
3 = Troisième doigt **4** = Quatrième doigt

Explication sur la Tablature
La tablature est un système de notation qui représente graphiquement les cordes et les frettes de la position de doigts de la guitare. Chaque note est indiquée en plaçant un chiffre, qui indique la frette ou la position des doigts à être placés, sur la corde appropriée. Par exemple:

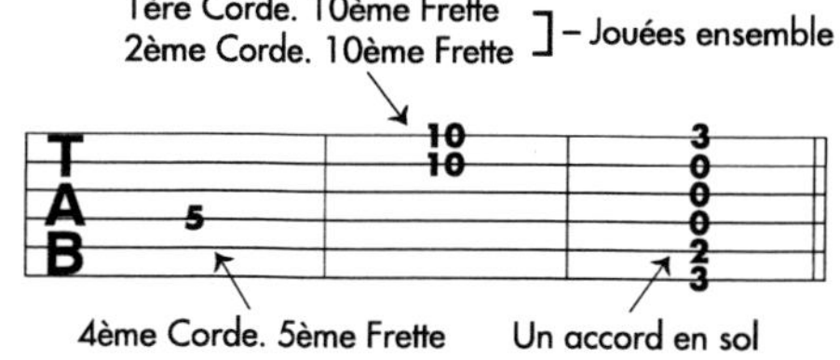

Miniature Overture

*Original key B♭ major

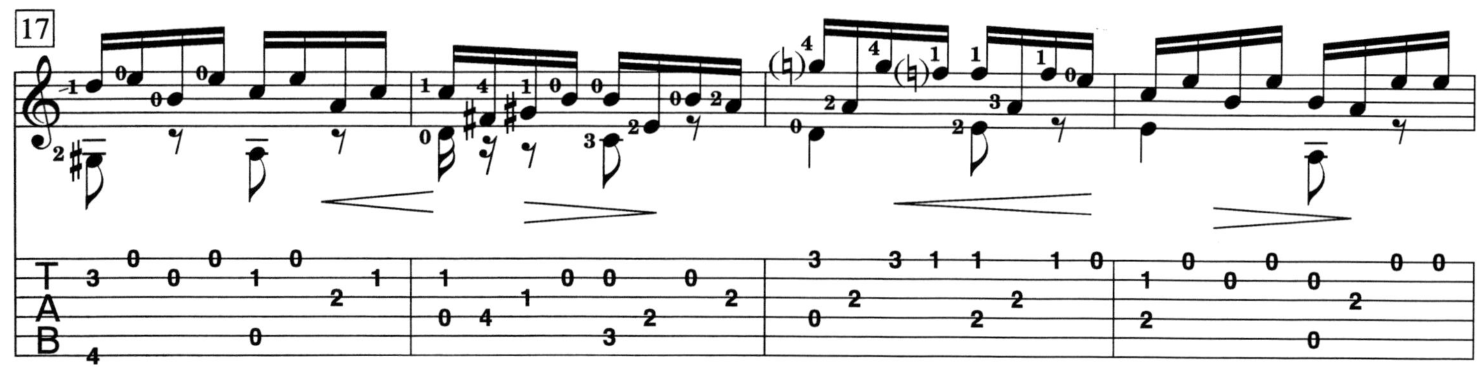
17
TAB

Pos. VII
Pos. II
Pos. I
21
p
p
TAB

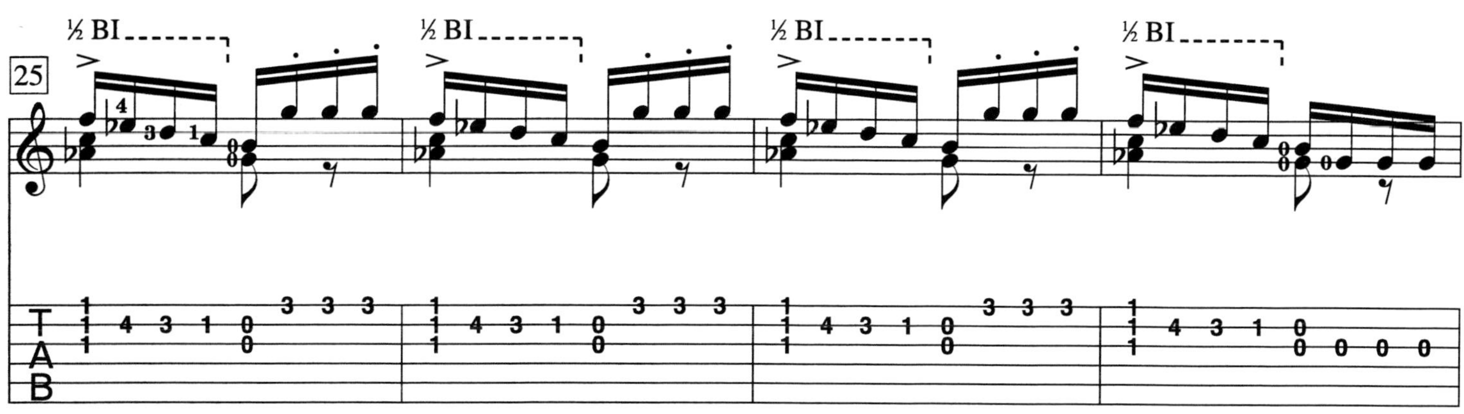
½ BI
½ BI
½ BI
½ BI
25
TAB

BI
29
p
cresc.
TAB

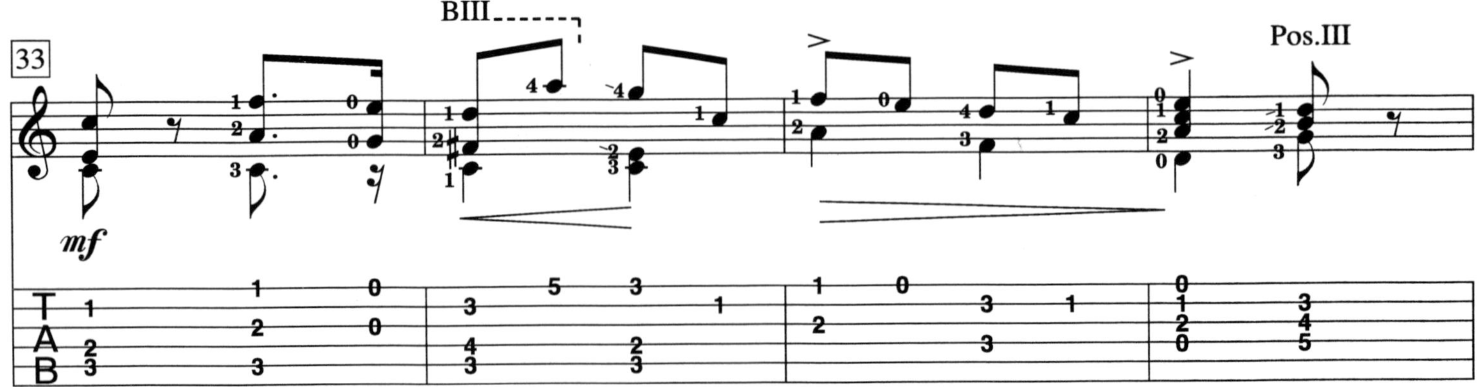
33
BIII
Pos.III
mf

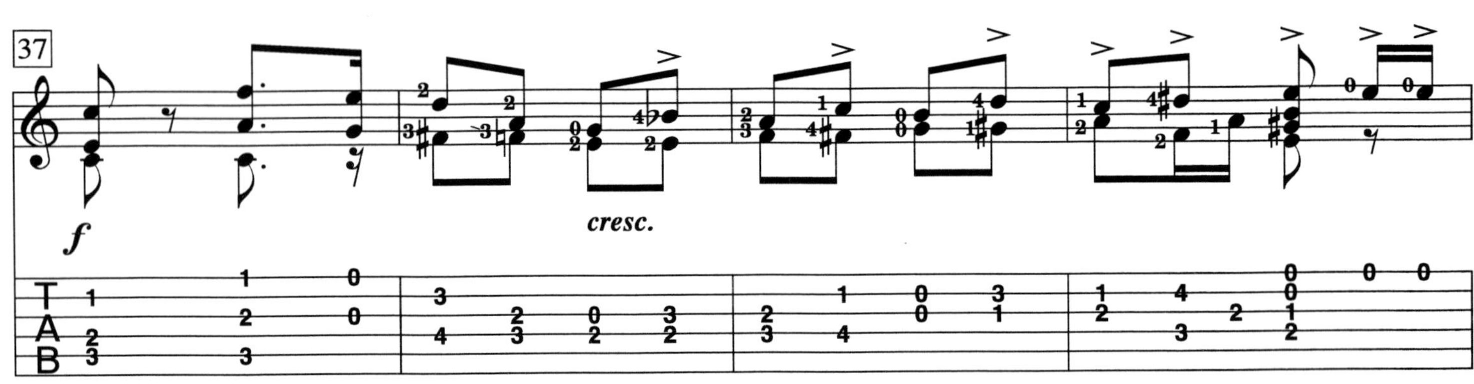
37
f
cresc.

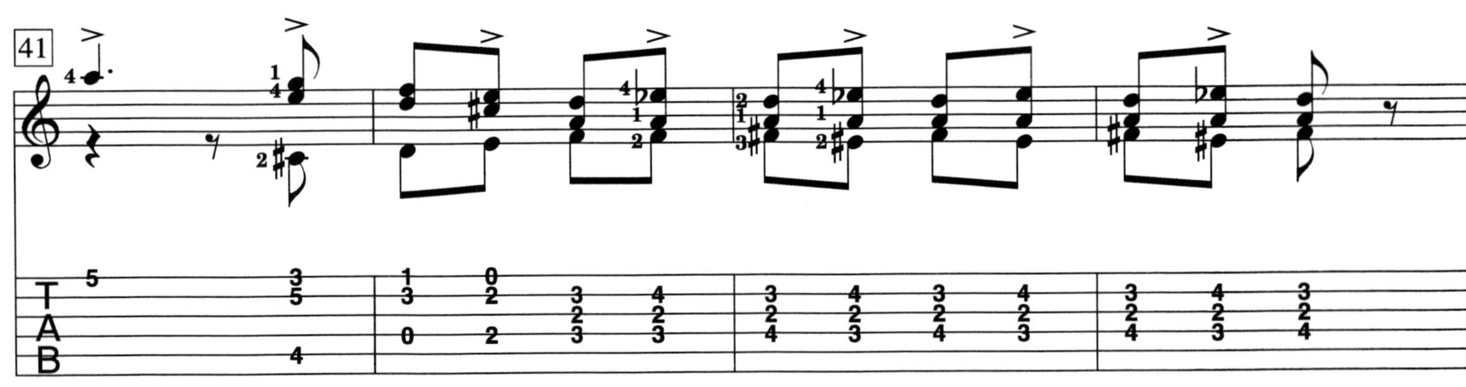
41

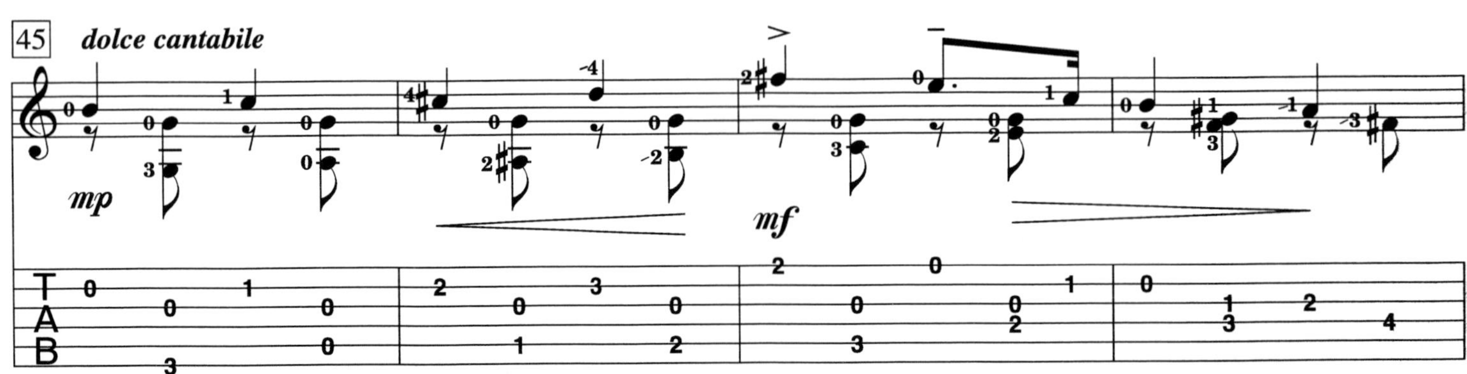
45
dolce cantabile
mp
mf

49
p
con grazia
p

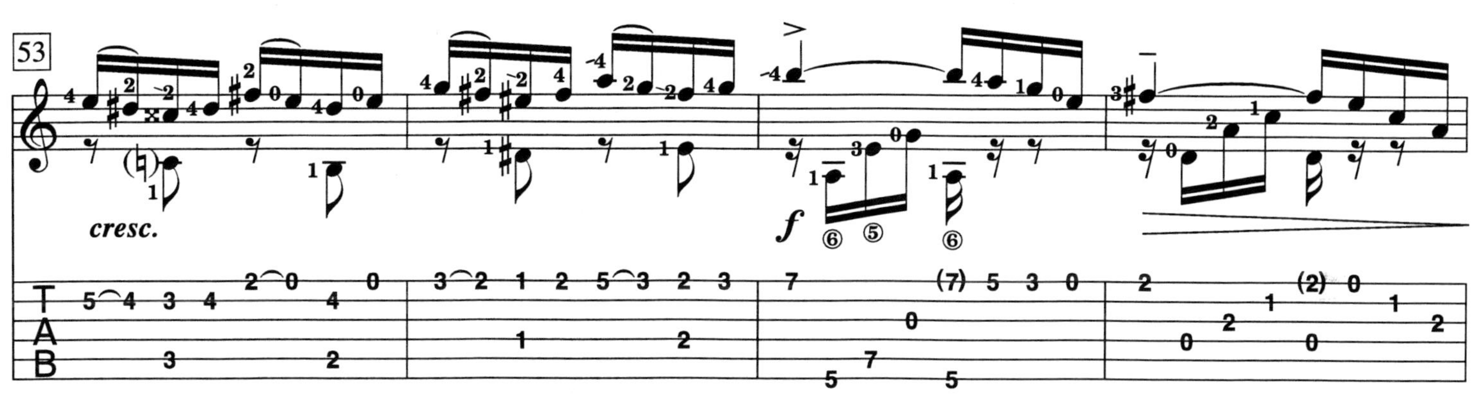
53
cresc.
f

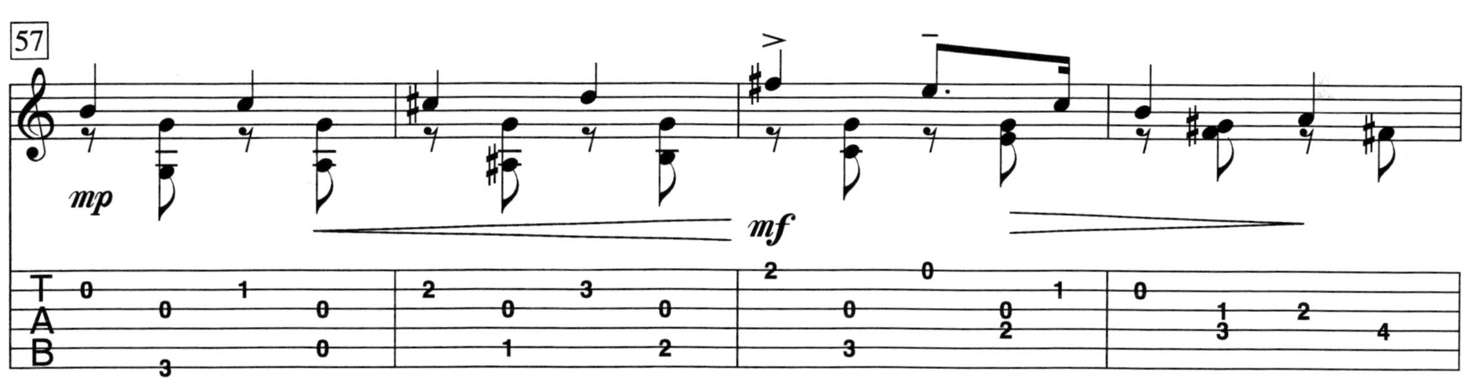
57
mp
mf

61
p
mp
p

65
mp
mf
TAB

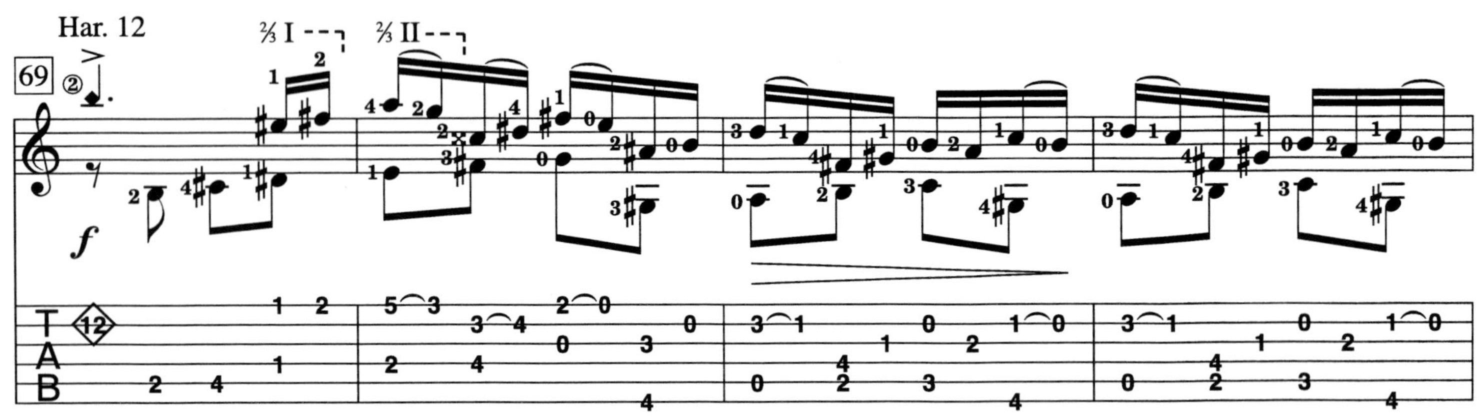
Har. 12
⅔ I
⅔ II
69
f
TAB

BIII
73
pp
cresc.
TAB

77
ff
pesante
TAB

81
brillante
f
TAB

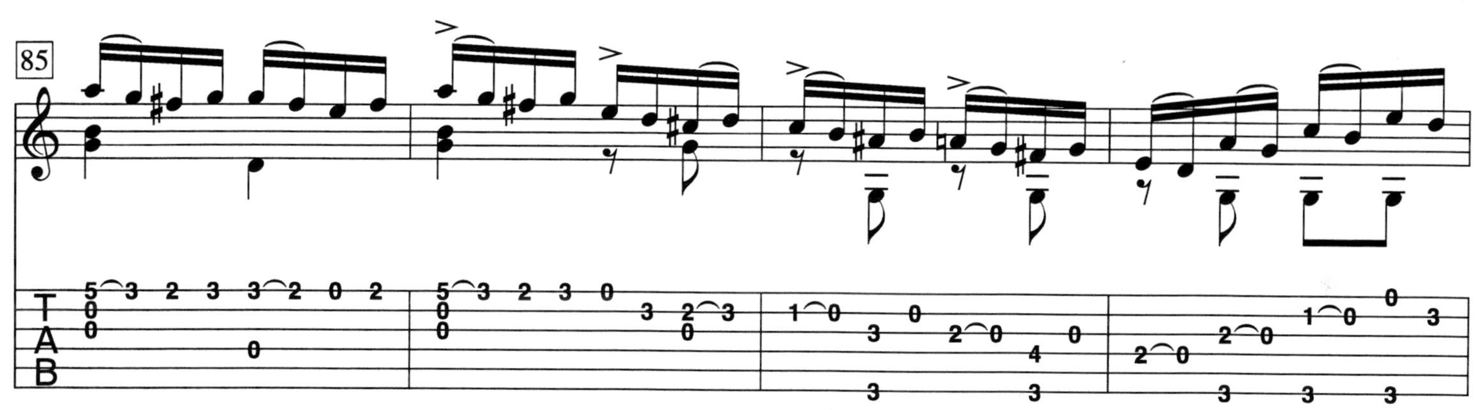
85
TAB

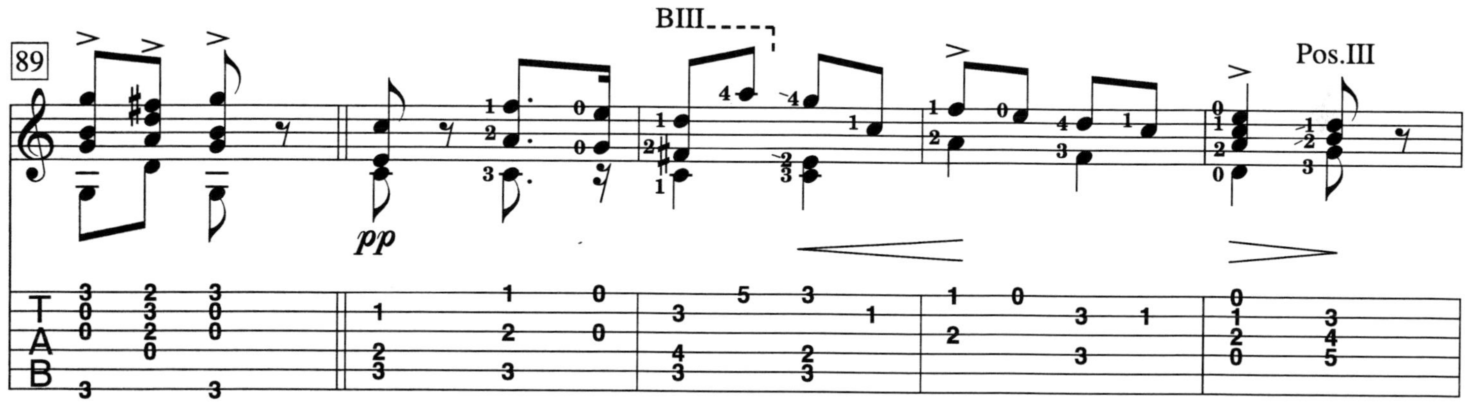
89
BIII
Pos.III
pp
TAB

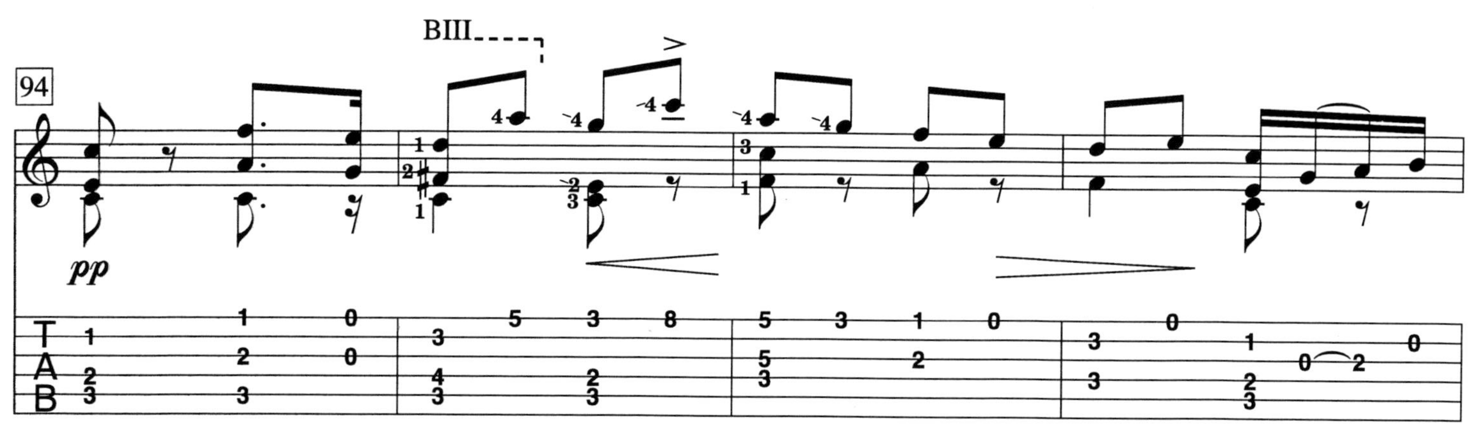
94
BIII
pp
TAB

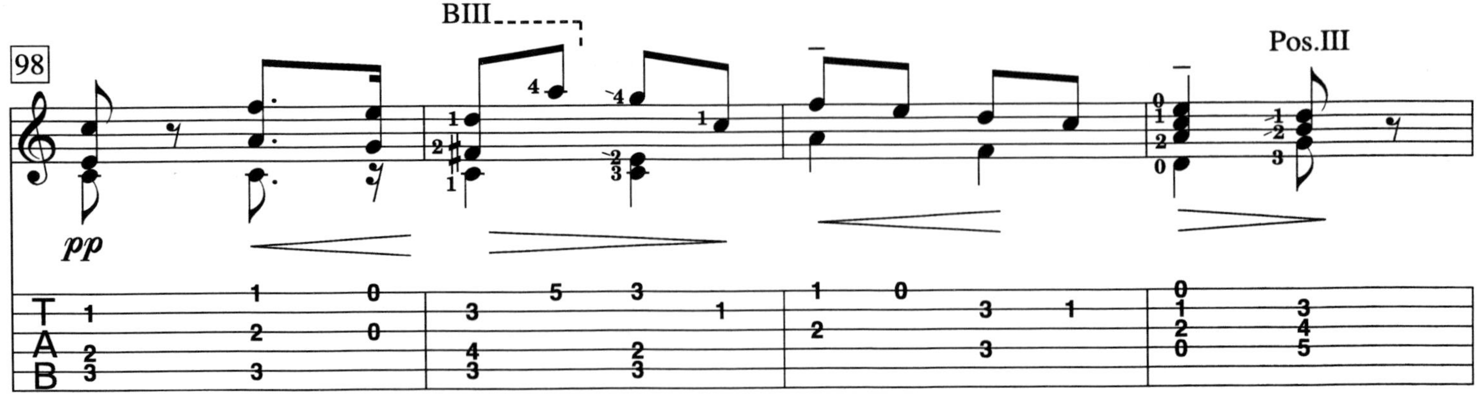
98
BIII
Pos.III
pp

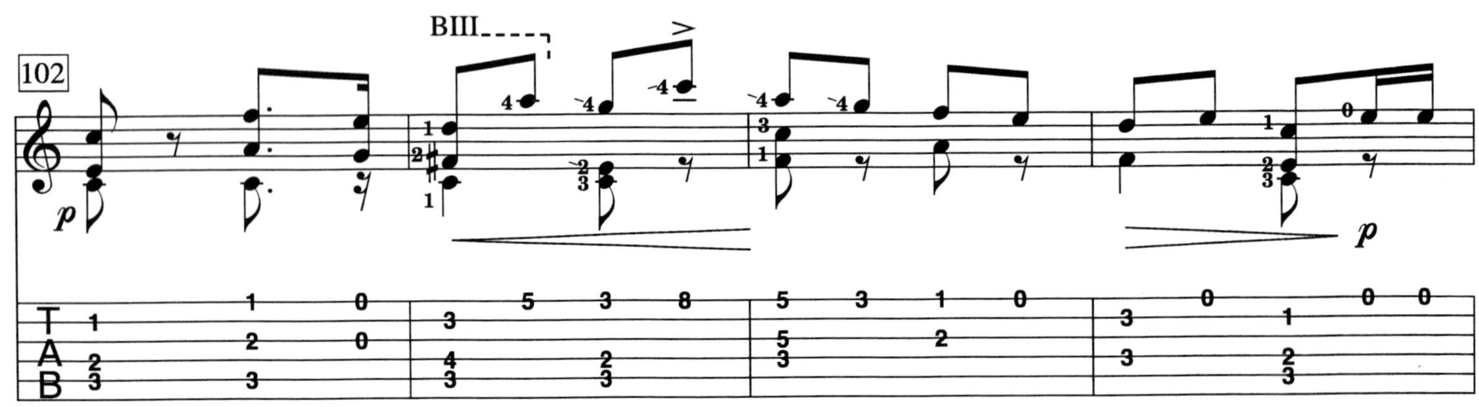
102
BIII
p
p

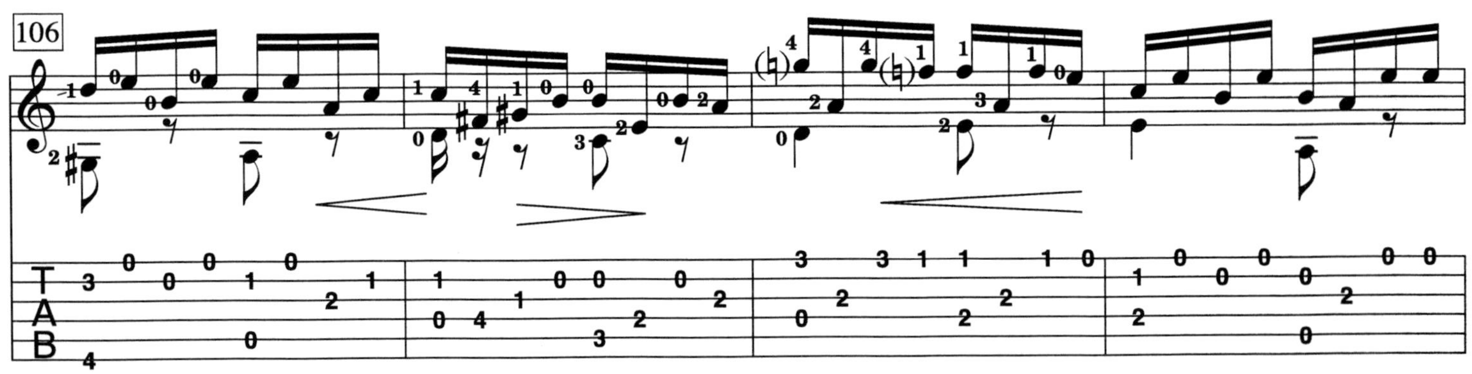
106

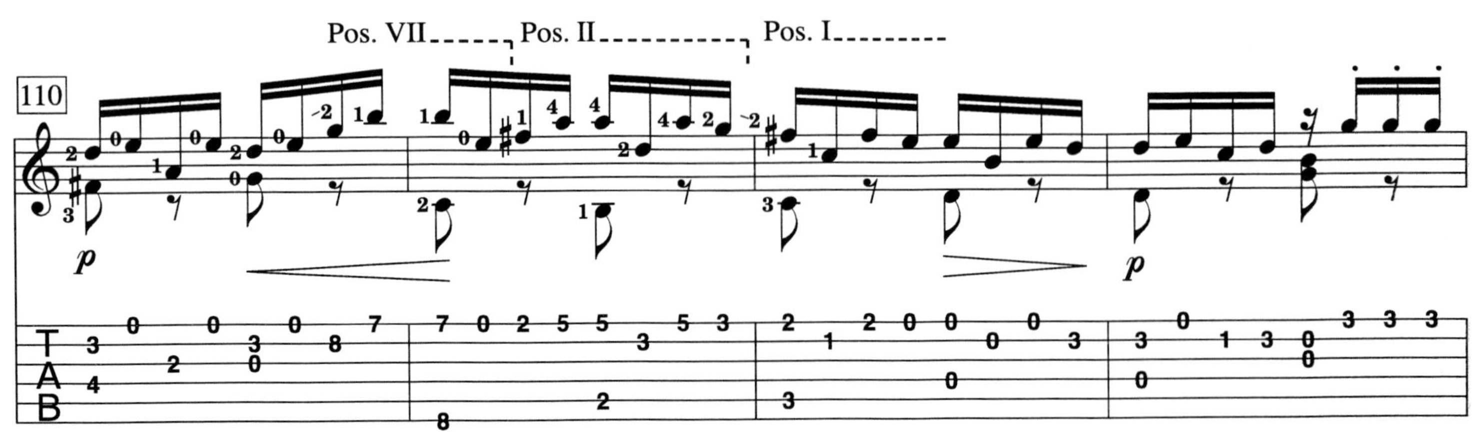
110
Pos. VII
Pos. II
Pos. I
p
p

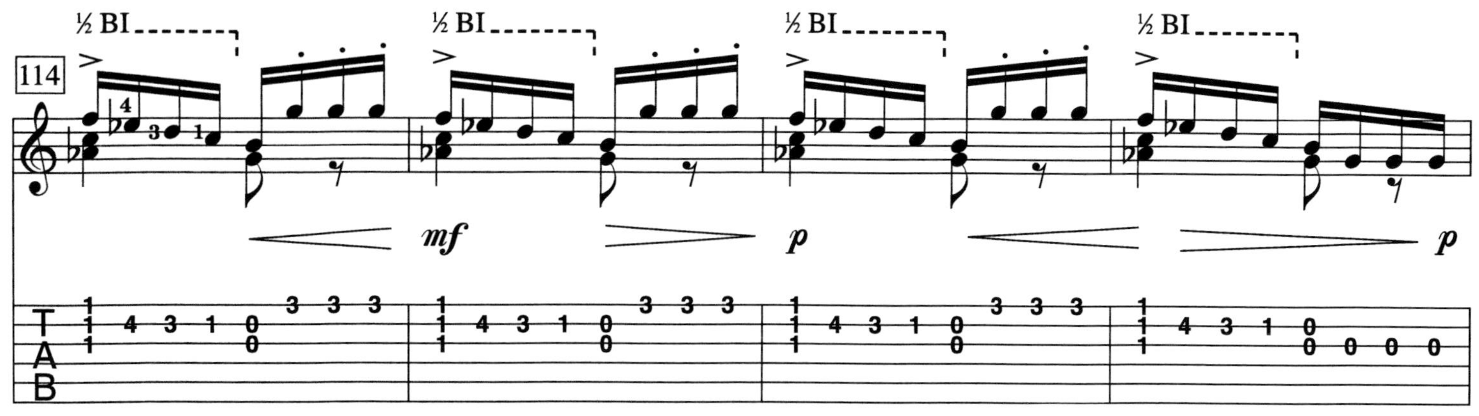
114
½ BI
½ BI
½ BI
½ BI
mf
p
p
T
A
B

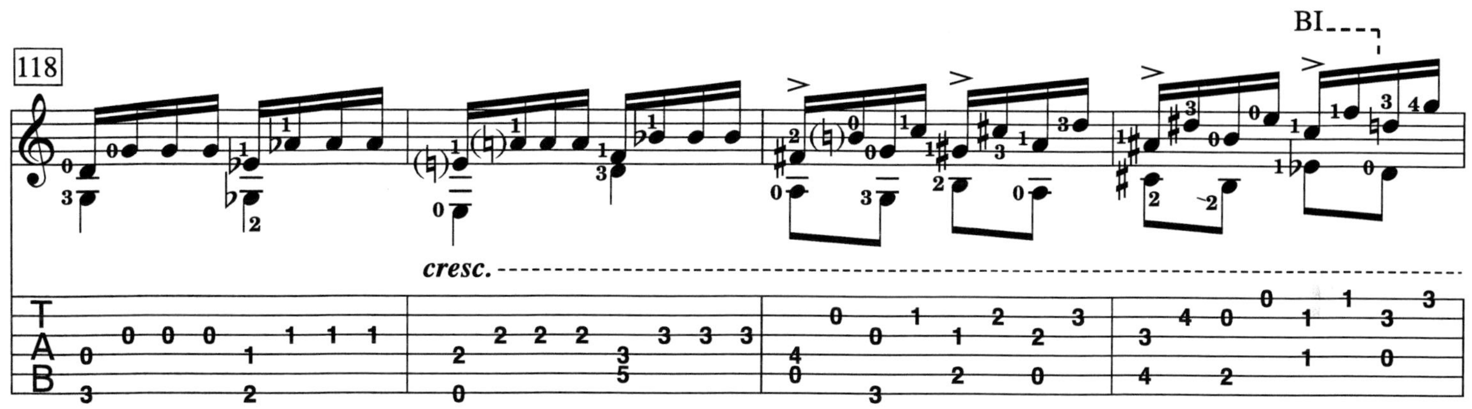
118
BI
cresc.
T
A
B

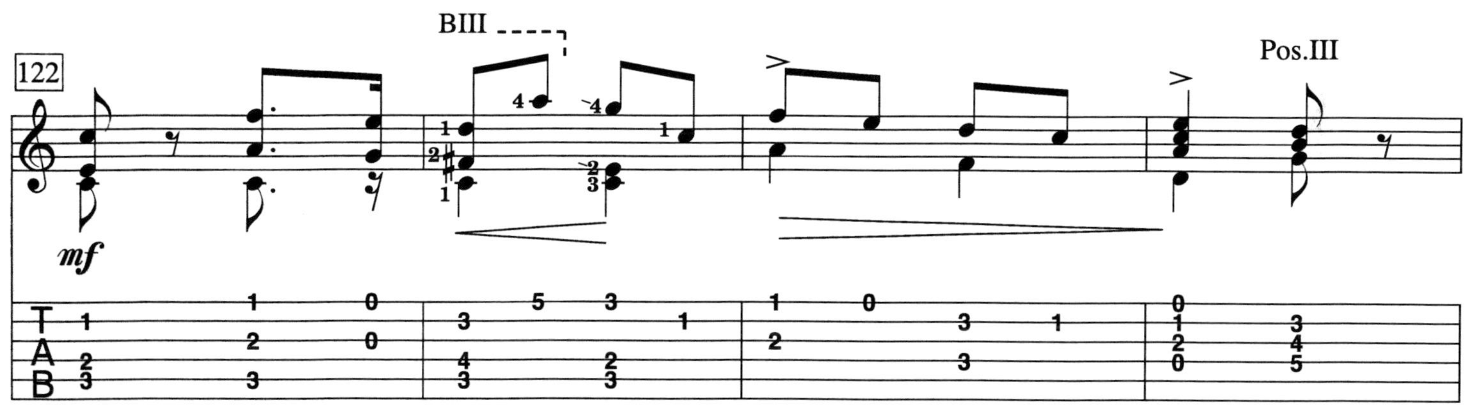
122
BIII
Pos.III
mf
T
A
B

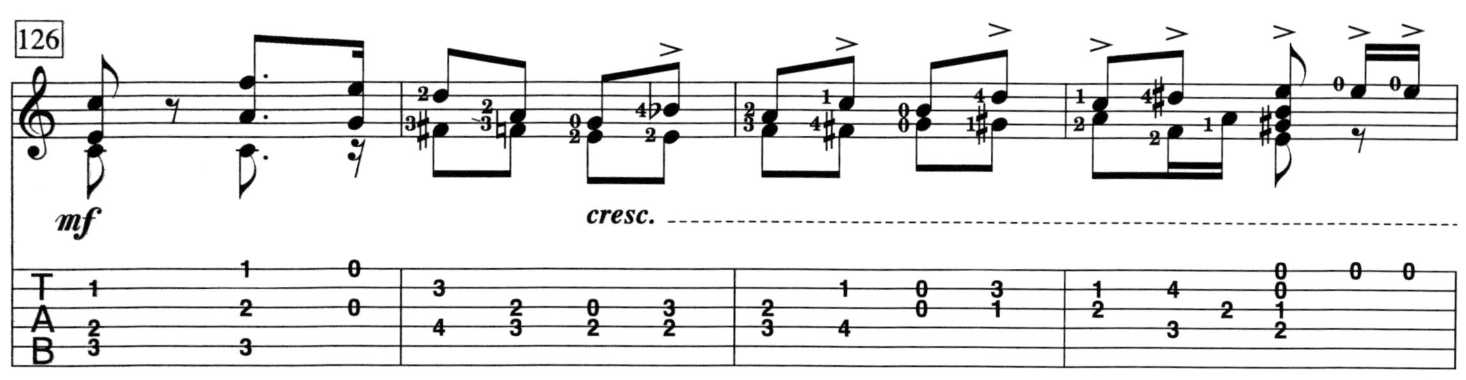
126
mf
cresc.
T
A
B

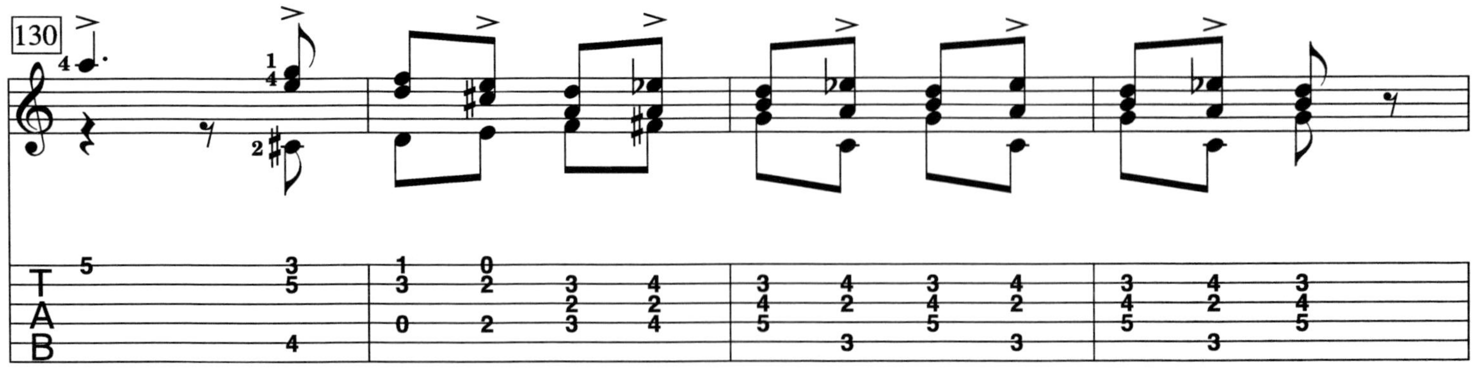
130

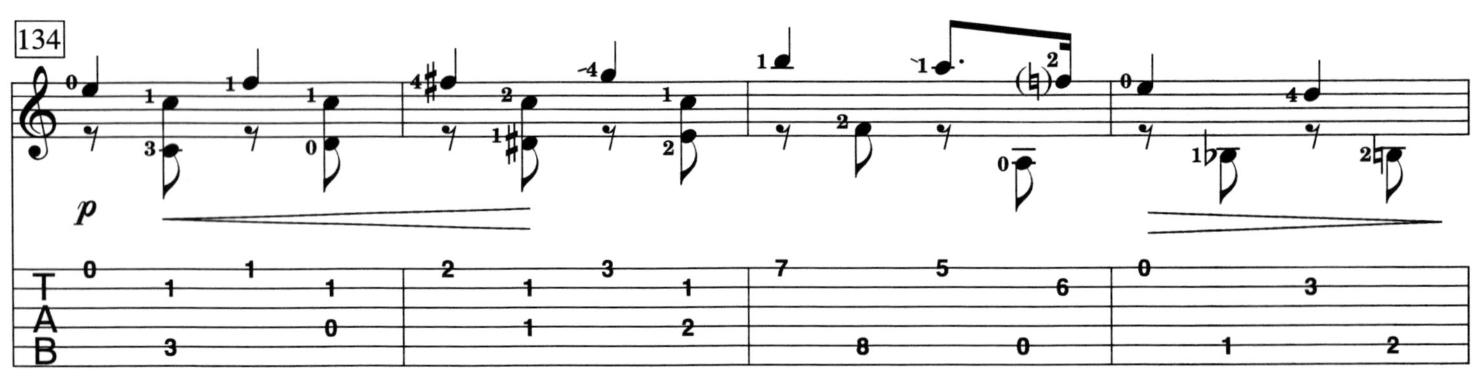
134
p

138
p
con grazia
p
cresc.

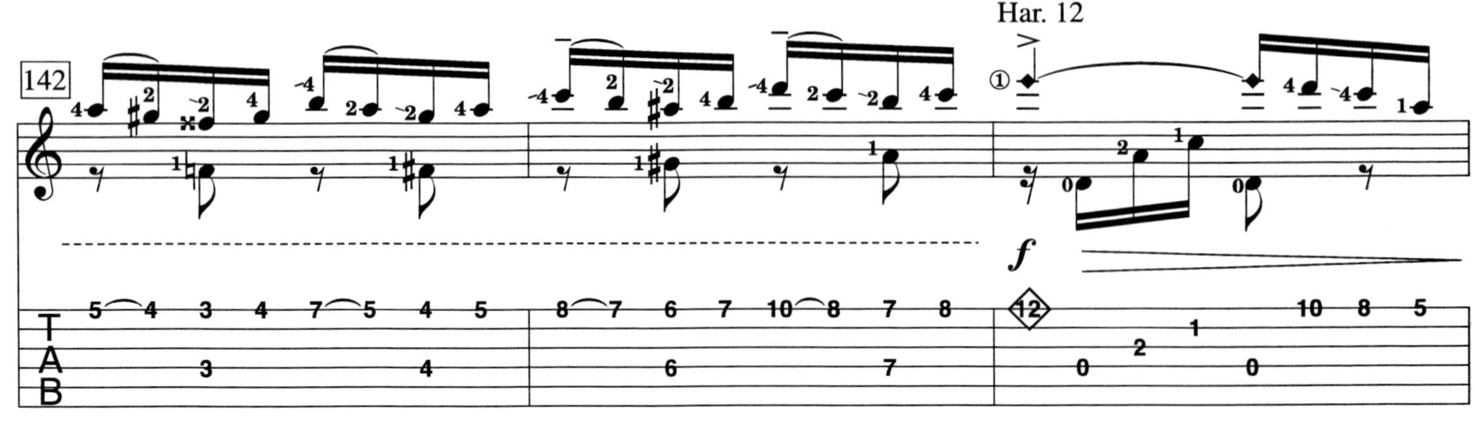
142
Har. 12
f

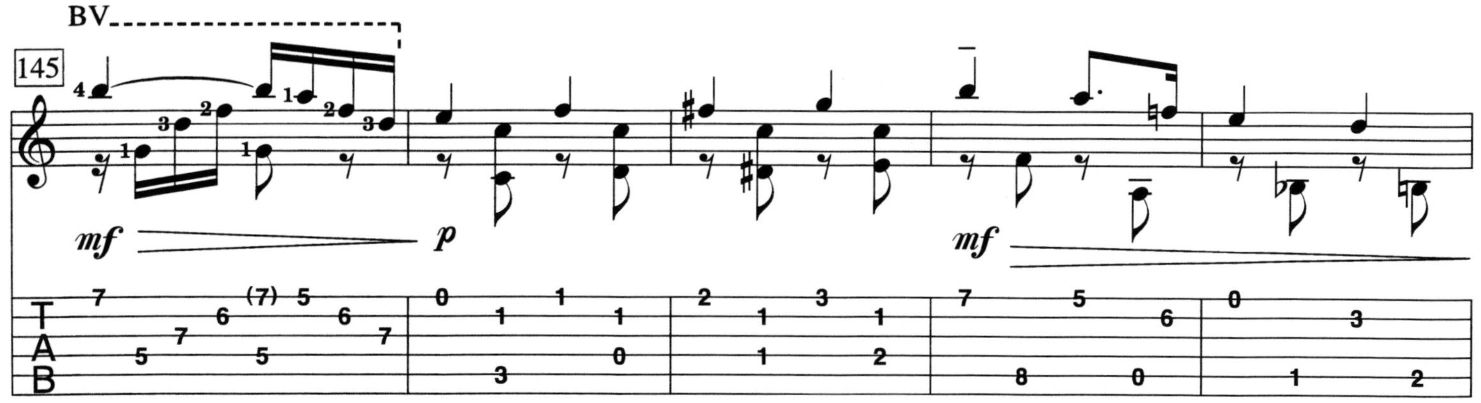
BV
145
mf
p
mf
TAB

150
p
p
TAB

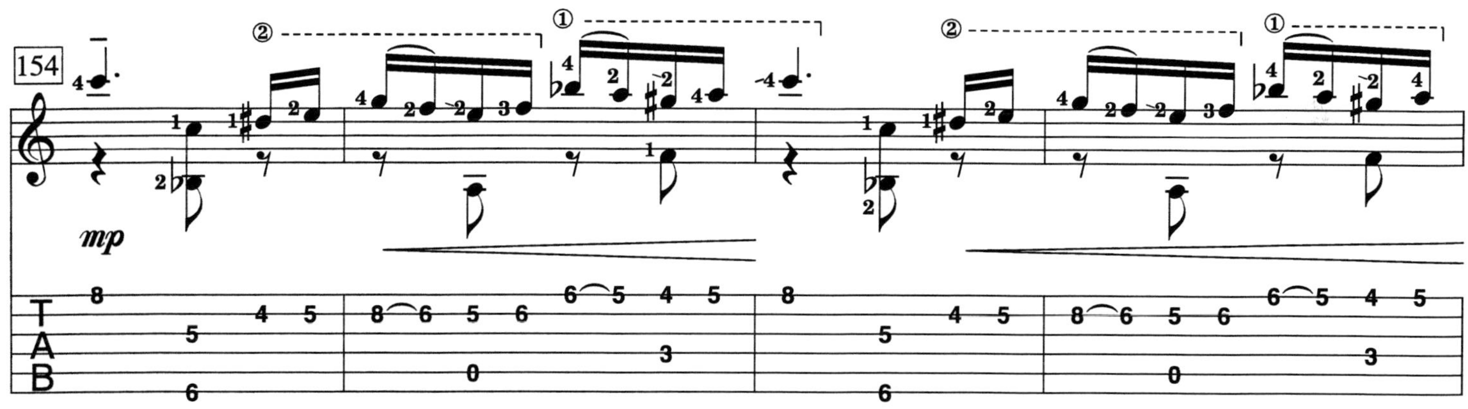
154
mp
TAB

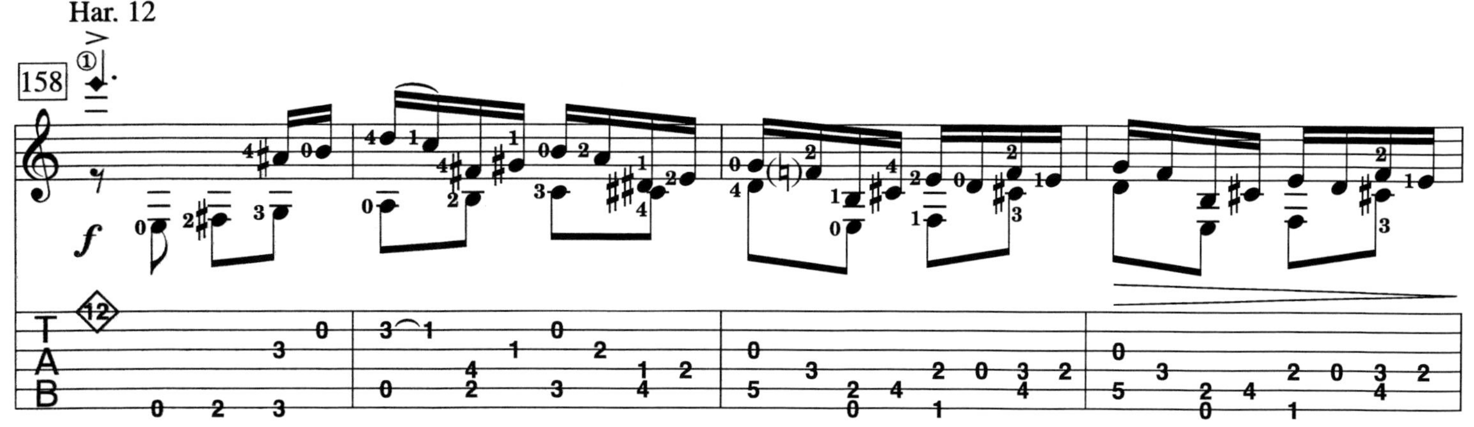
Har. 12
158
f
TAB

162
pp
cresc.
166
ff
170
sempre ff
174
178
sfz
sfz

March

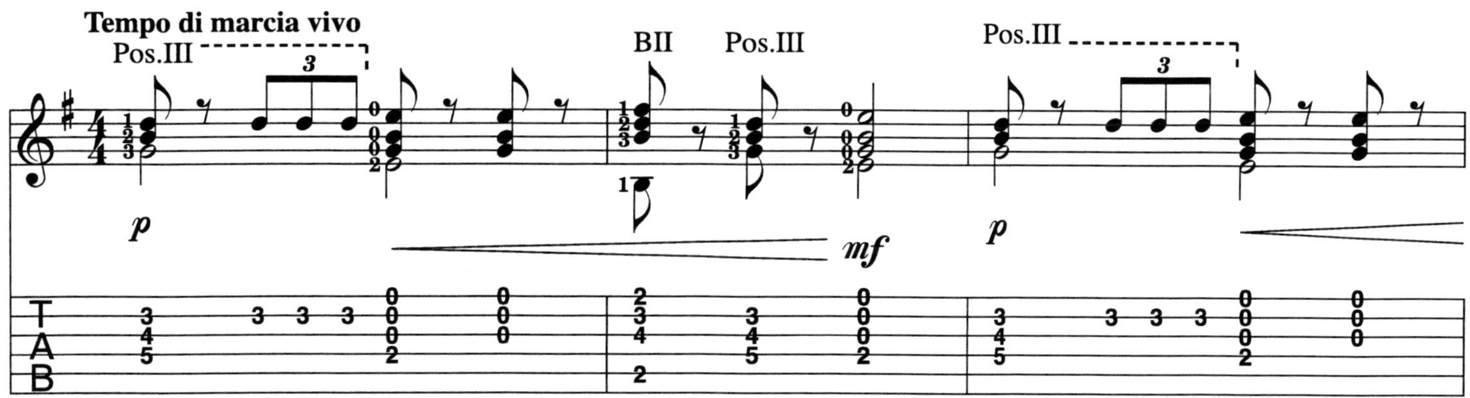
Tempo di marcia vivo
Pos.III
BII
Pos.III
Pos.III
p
mf
p

4
BII
Pos.III
mf
p

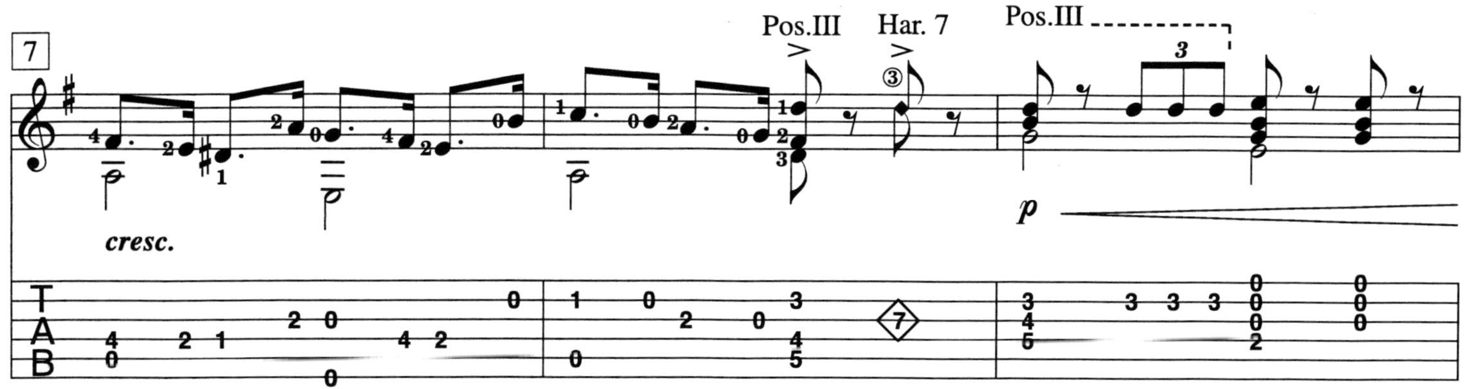
7
Pos.III
Har. 7
Pos.III
cresc.
p

10
BII
Pos.III
Pos.III
BII
Pos.III
mf
p
mf
p

13
cresc.
mf
TAB

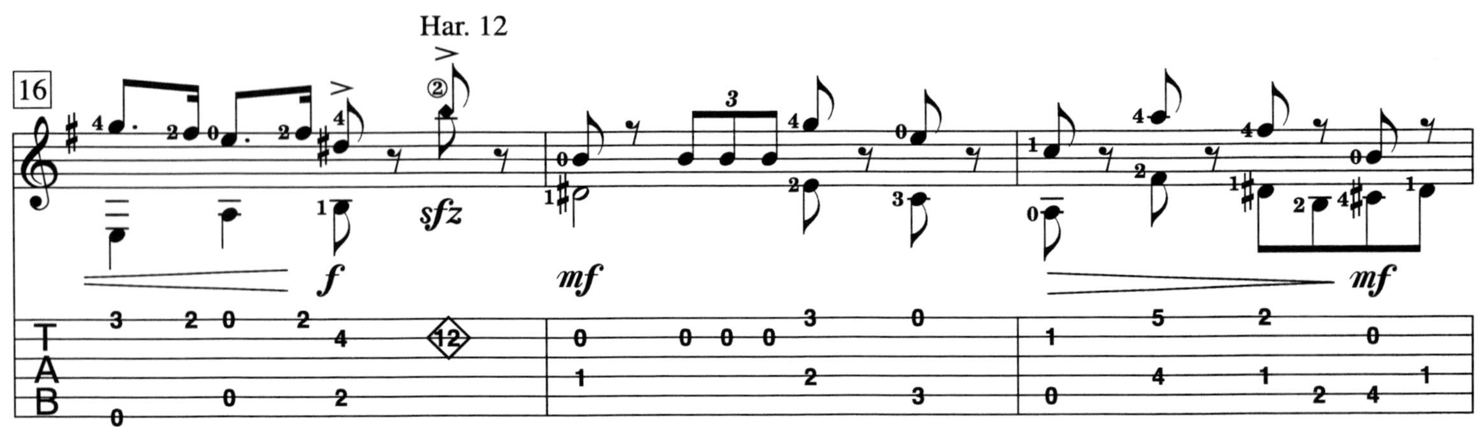
Har. 12
16
sfz
f
mf
mf
TAB

19
f
mf
TAB

Pos.III
22
mf
f
TAB

25
Pos.III
BII
Pos.III
Pos.III
p
mf
p
28
BII
Pos.III
mf
p
31
Pos.III
Har. 7
Pos.III
cresc.
p
34
BII
Pos.III
Pos.III
BII
Pos.III
mf
p
mf
p
38
cresc.
f
sfz
Fine

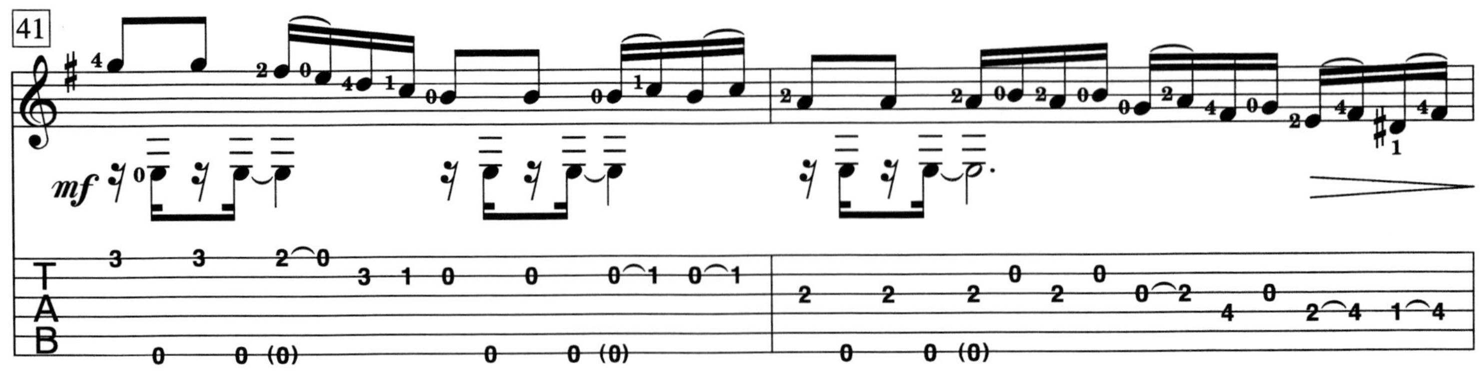
41
mf

43
mp
f

45
mf

47
D.C. al Fine
mp
f

Dance of the Sugar Plum Fairy

*Original meter $\frac{2}{4}$

to Coda
17
TAB

20
½ BII
sfz
pp
p
TAB

23
½ BII
sfz
pp
TAB

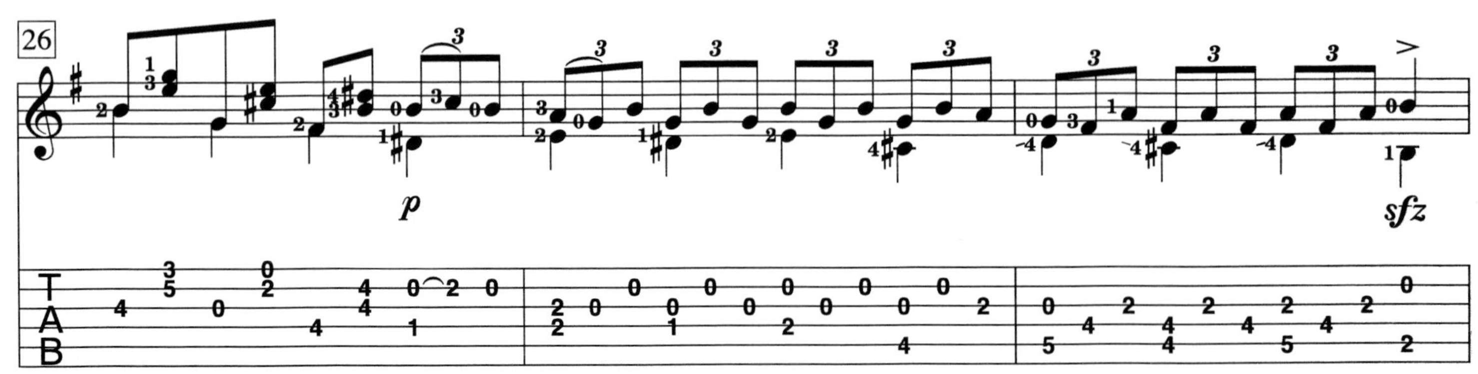
26
p
sfz
TAB

29
½ BII
p
sfz
p
sfz
p
cresc.
TAB

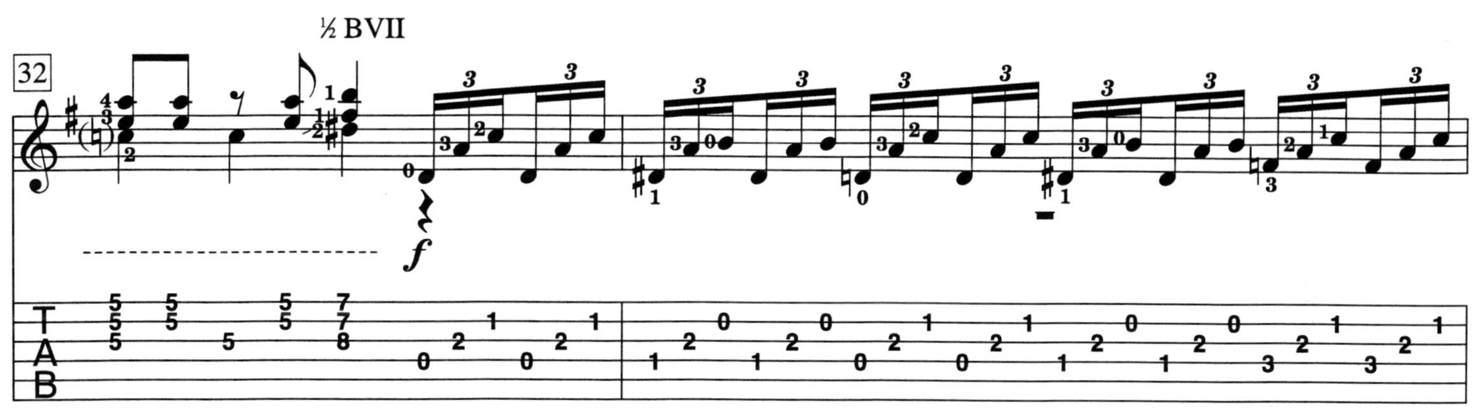
32
½ BVII
f
TAB

34
½ BII
½ BVII
TAB

36
D.S. al Coda
decresc.
p
TAB

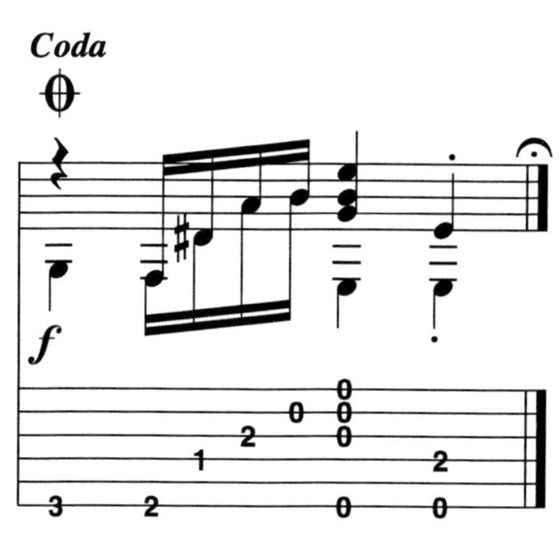
Coda
f
TAB

Russian Dance

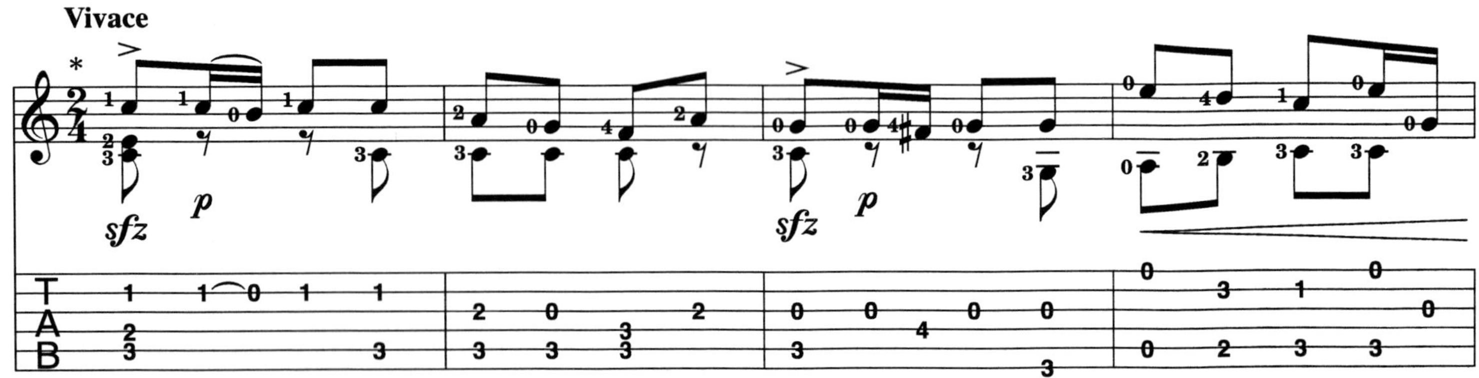

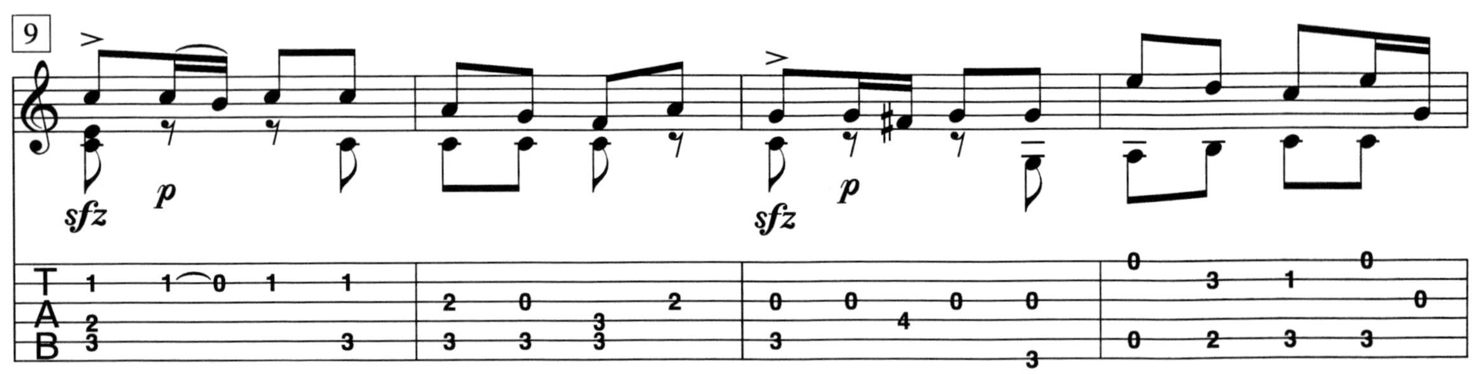

*Original key G major

17
sfz
mf
sfz
mf
21
cresc.
25
sfz
mf
sfz
mf
29
cresc.
ff
33
p
cresc.

37
ff
41
f
45
ff
½ BI
49
mf
ff
½ BI
mf
ff
½ BI
53
mf
ff
½ BI
ff
½ BI
½ BI
½ BI

57
sfz
mf
sffz
mf
61
f
stringendo cresc. poco a poco
65
69
ff
cresc.
Prestissimo
73
ff
cresc.
fff
sfz

Arabian Dance

⑥ = D

*Original key G minor, original meter 3/8

**Throughout the *Arabian Dance* this rhythmic figure may be simplified to

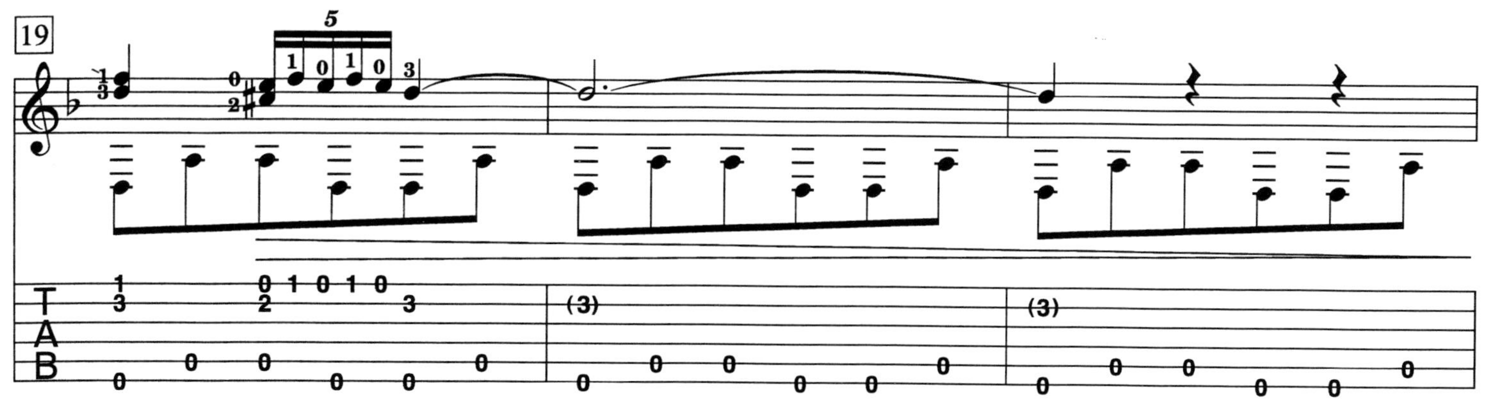
19

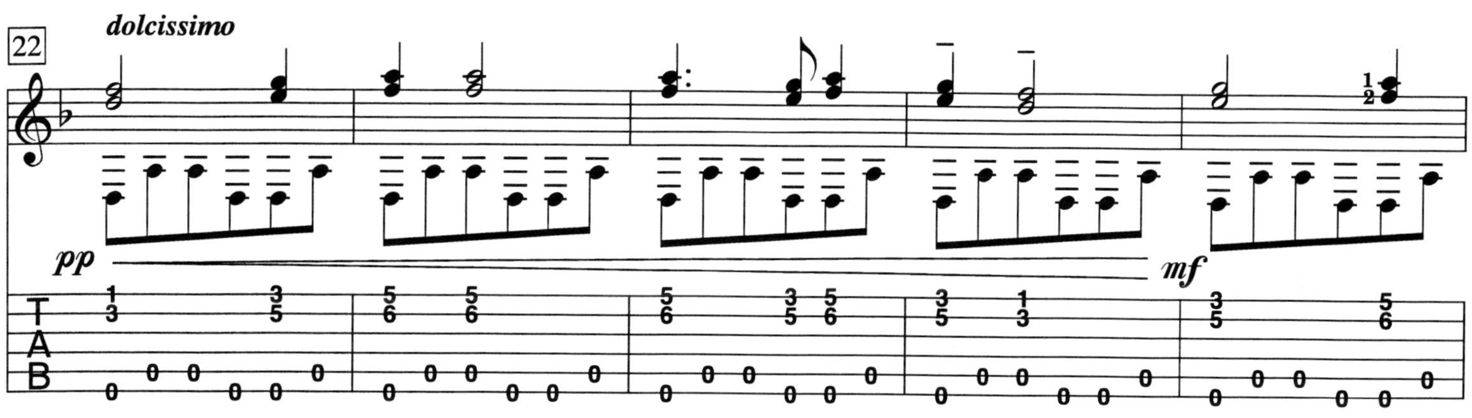
22
dolcissimo
pp
mf

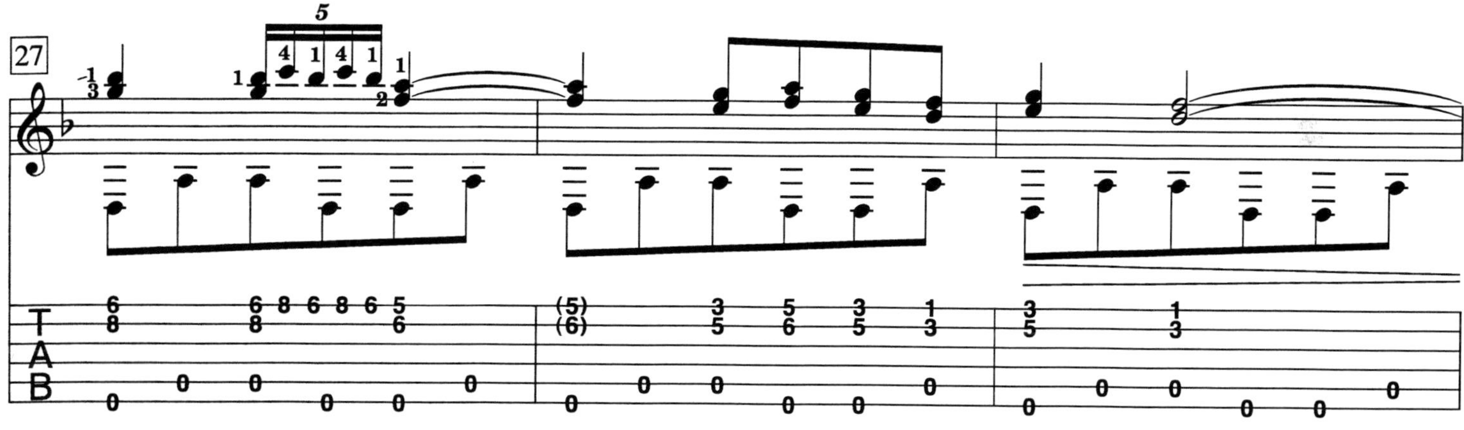
27

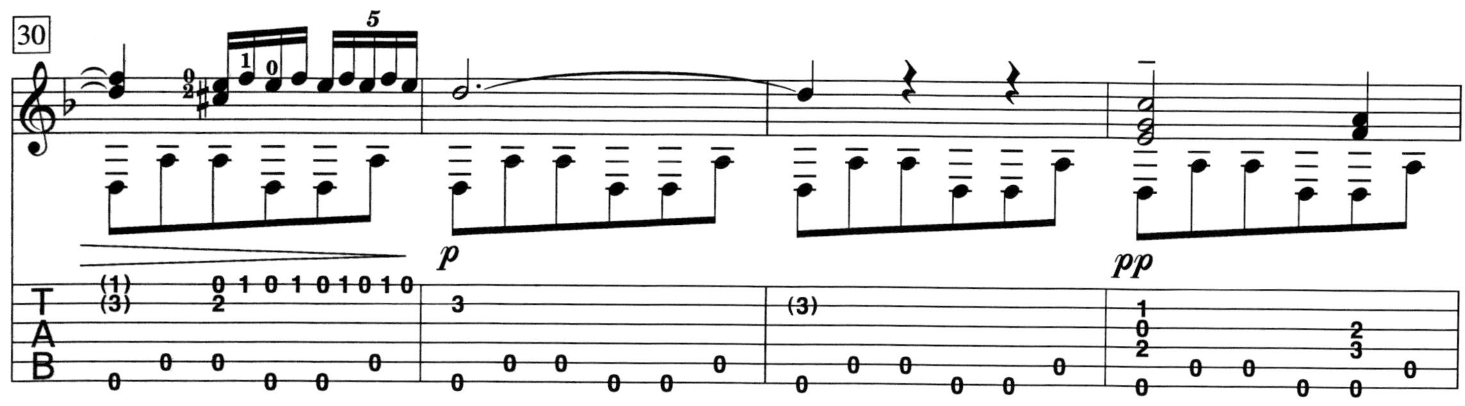
30
p
pp

34
pp
38
41
p
45
mf
48
p

52
mf
55
p
58
pp
63
p
67
pp
mf

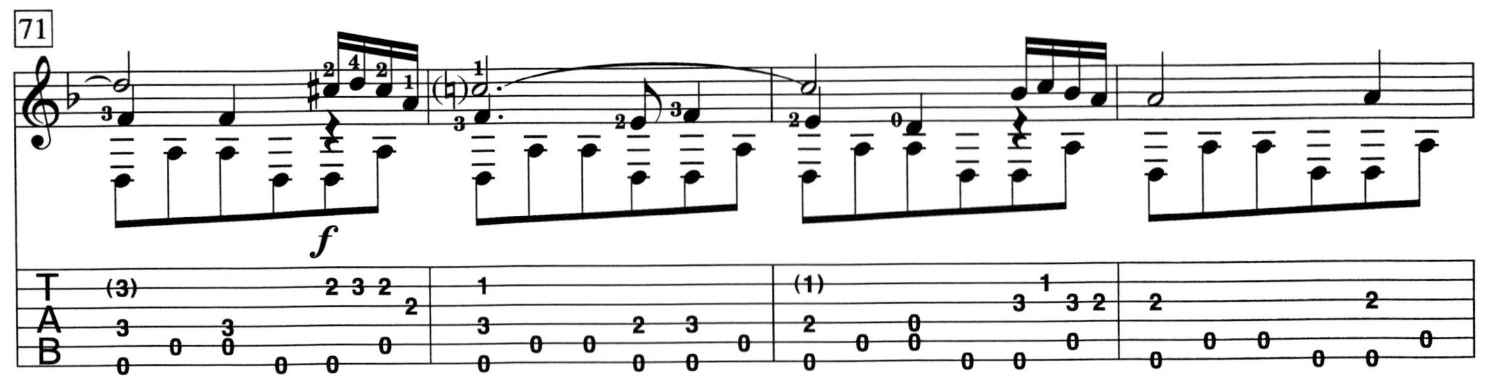
71
f
TAB

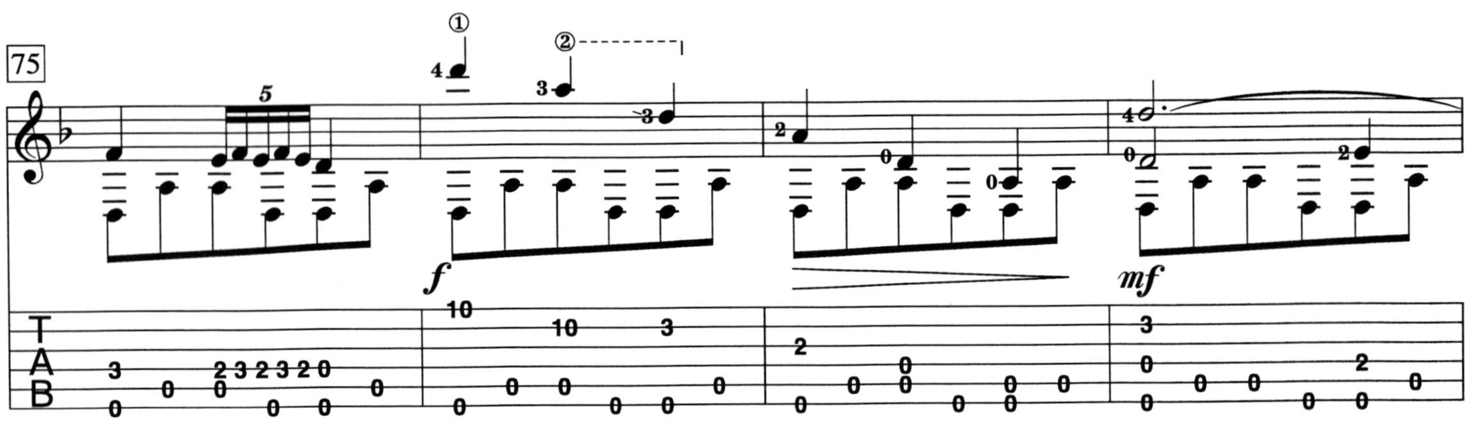
75
f
mf
TAB

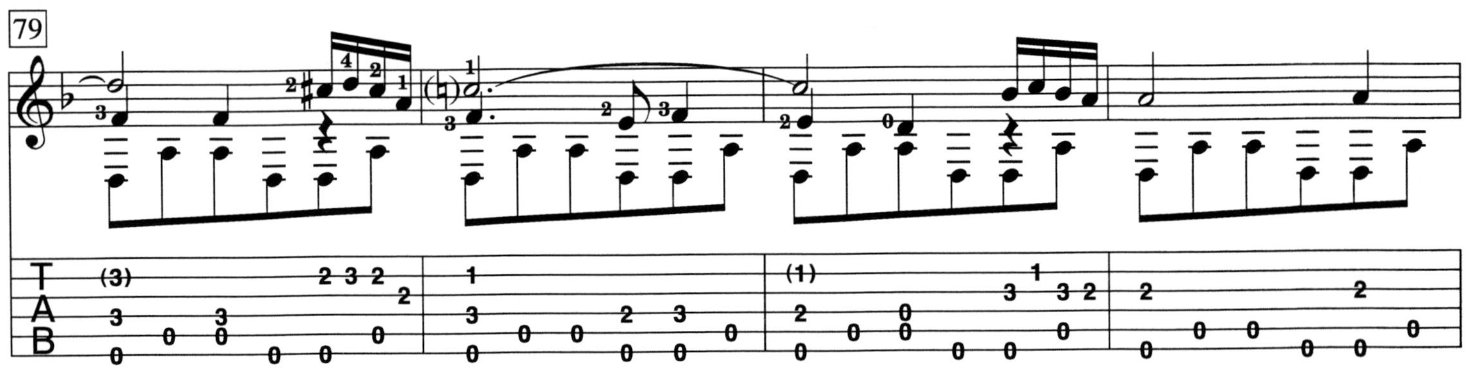
79
TAB

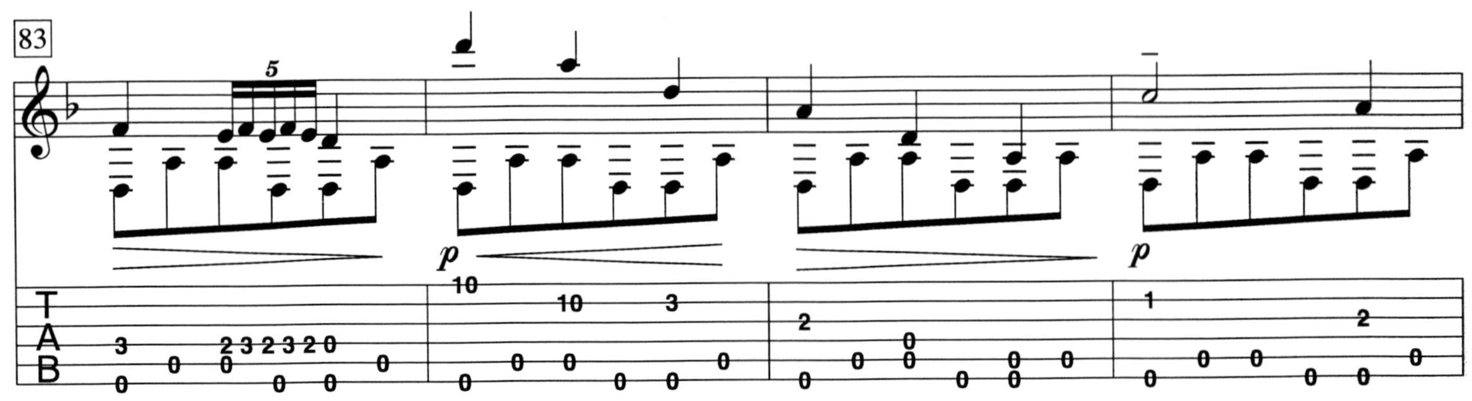
83
p
p
TAB

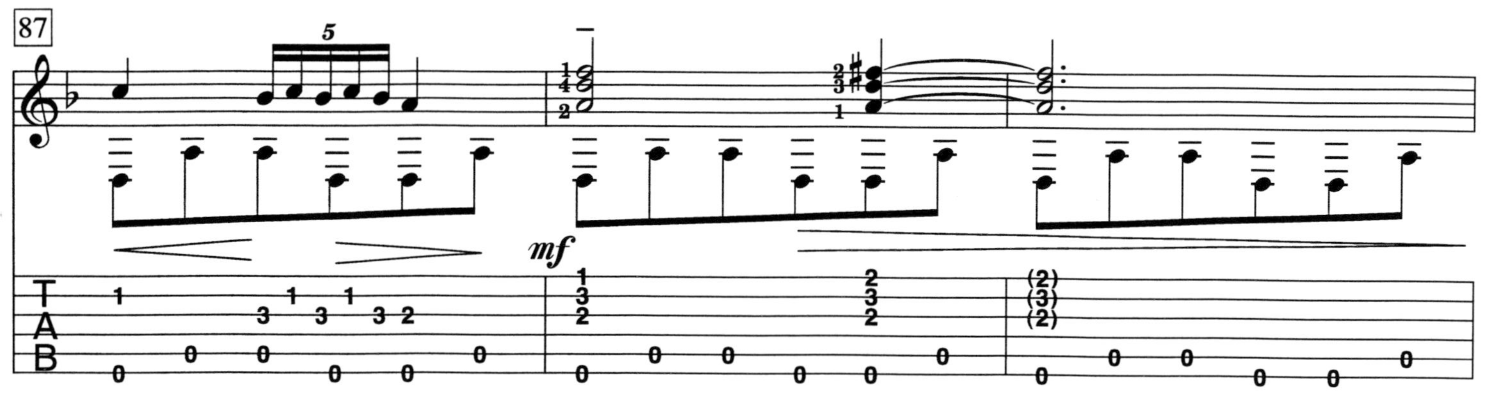

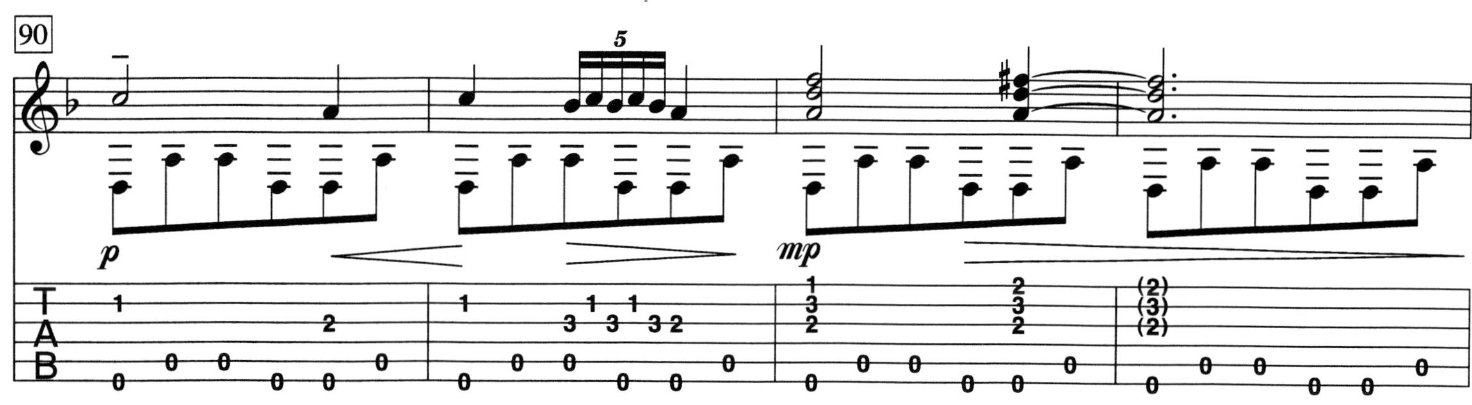

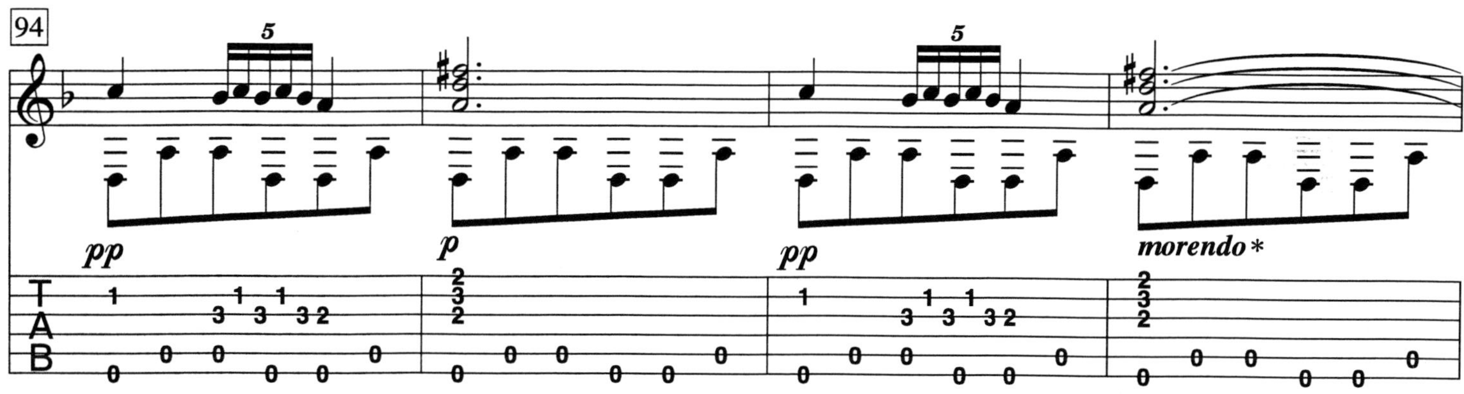

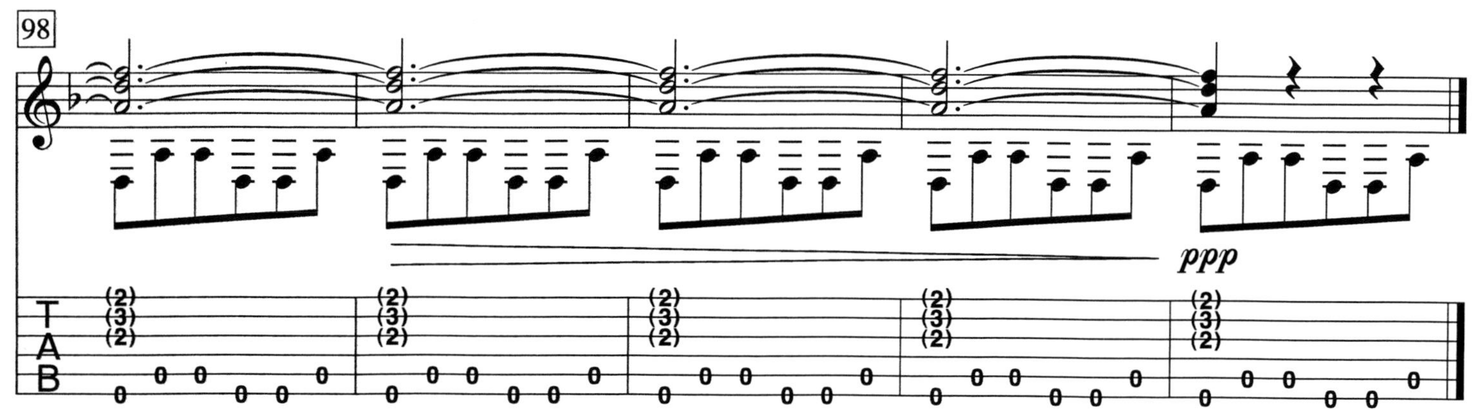

**Morendo* = dying away.

Chinese Dance

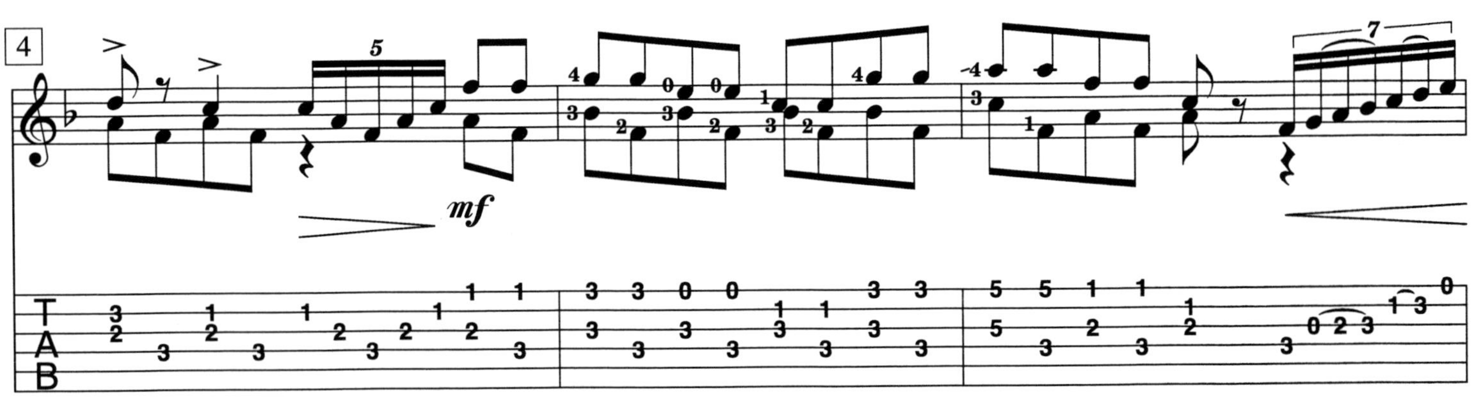

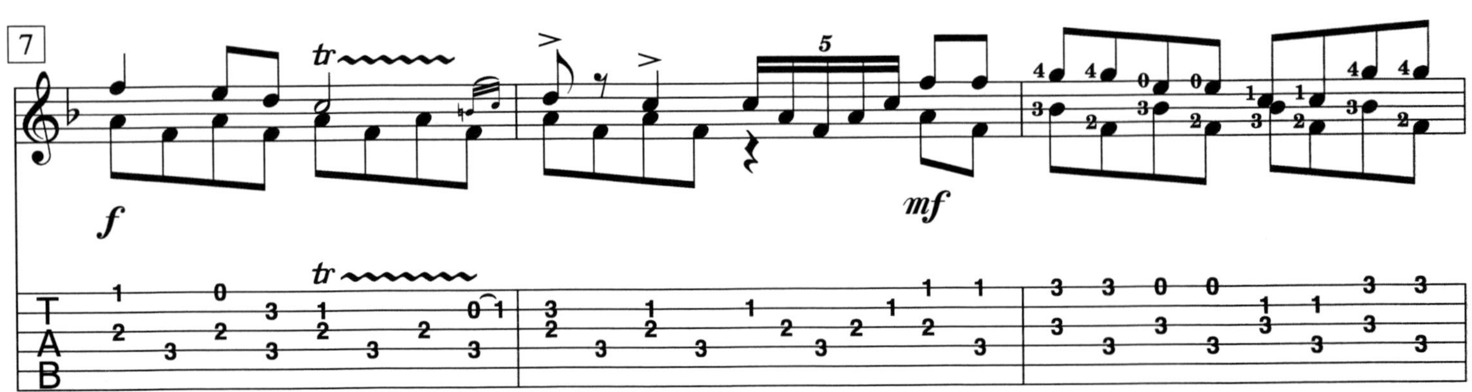

*Original key B♭ major

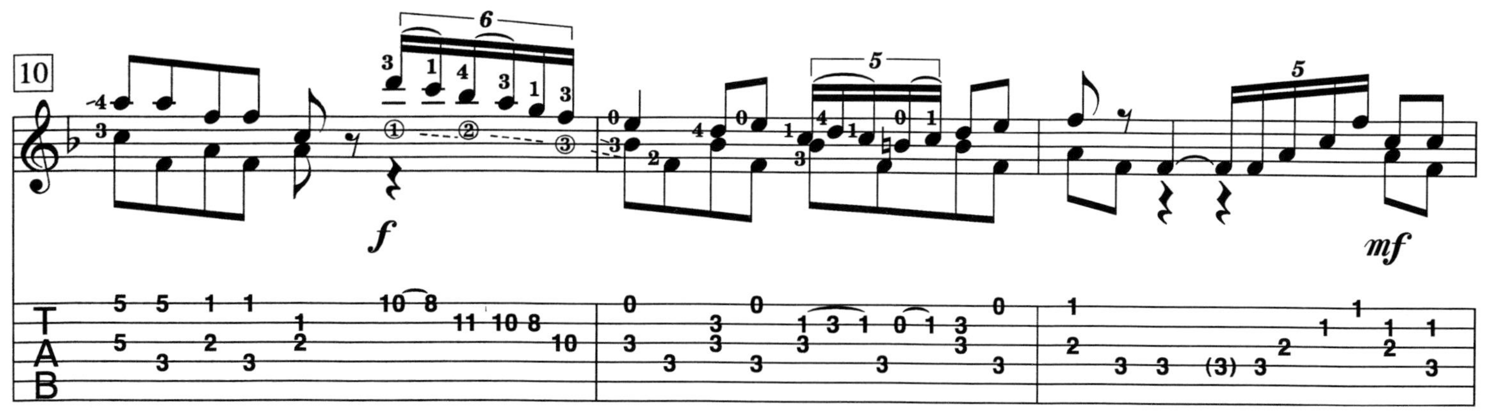
10
f
mf
T
A
B

BIII
13
f
T
A
B

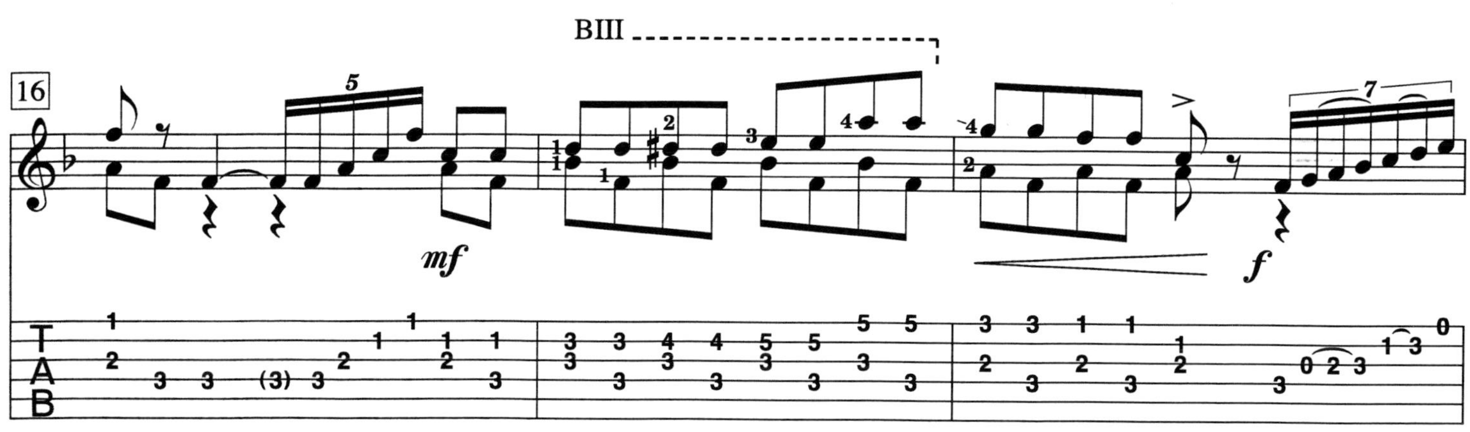
BIII
16
mf
f
T
A
B

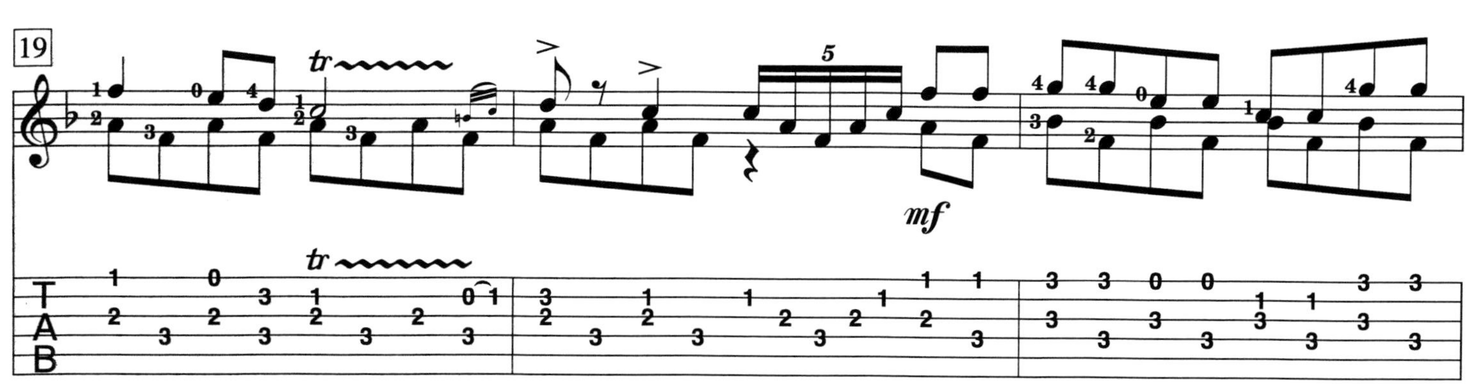
19
tr
mf
T
A
B

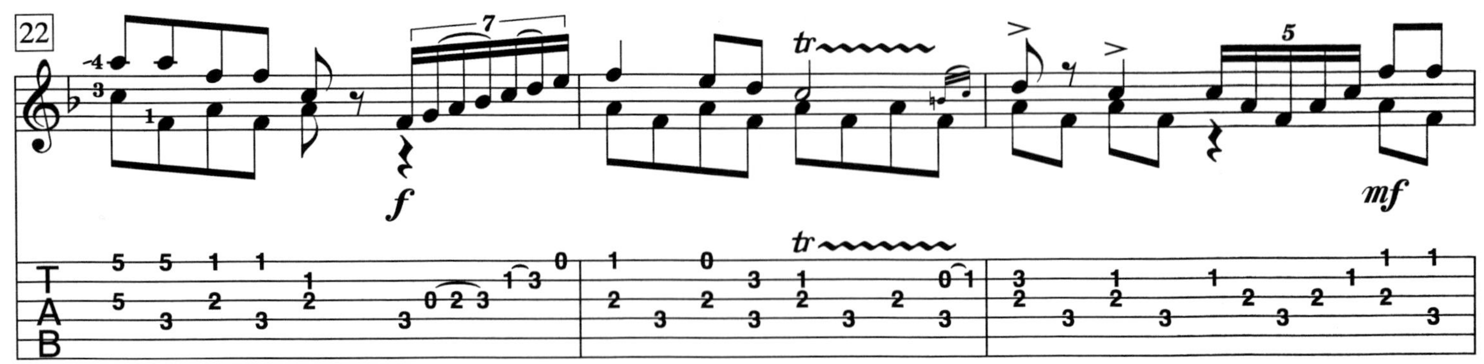
22
7
tr
5
f
mf
T
A
B

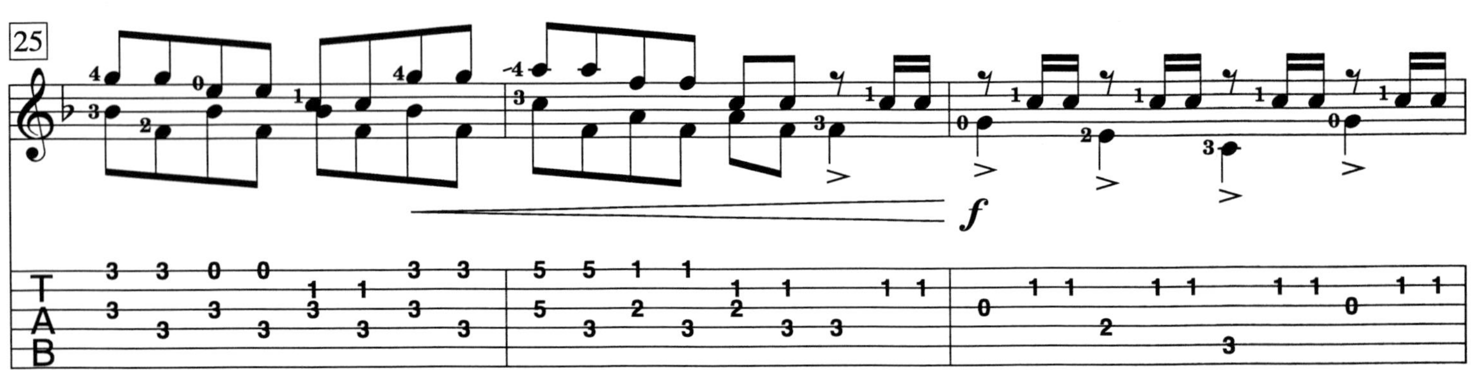
25
f
T
A
B

28
cresc.
T
A
B

30
ff
T
A
B

Dance of the Flutes

*Original meter 2/4

18
f
T
A
B

21
mf
p
T
A
B

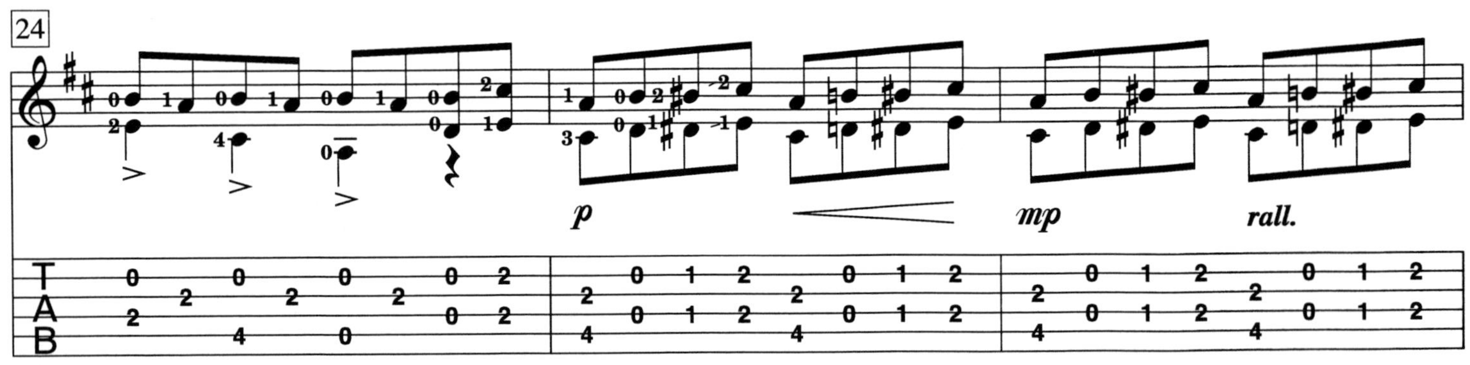
24
p
mp
rall.
T
A
B

27
p
mf
T
A
B

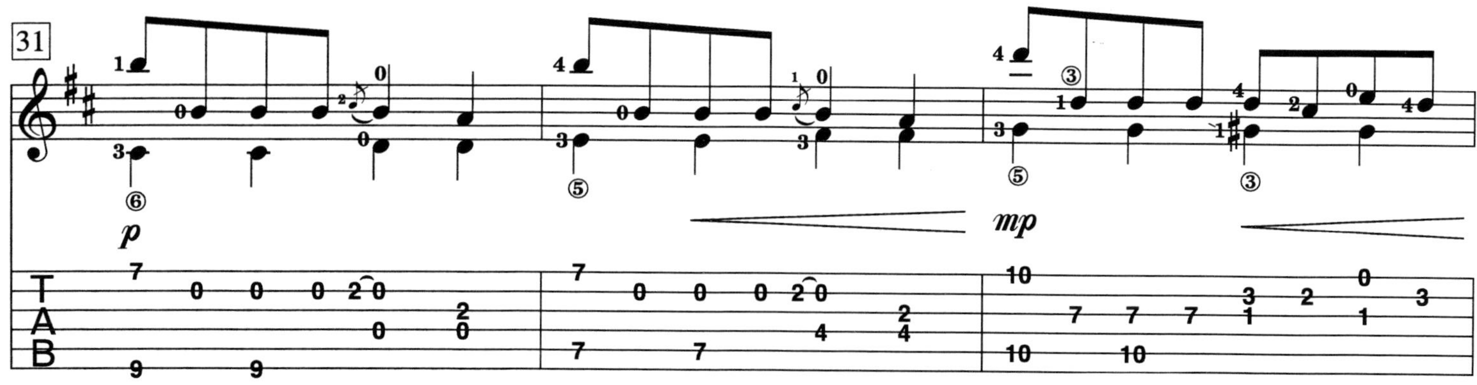
31
p
mp

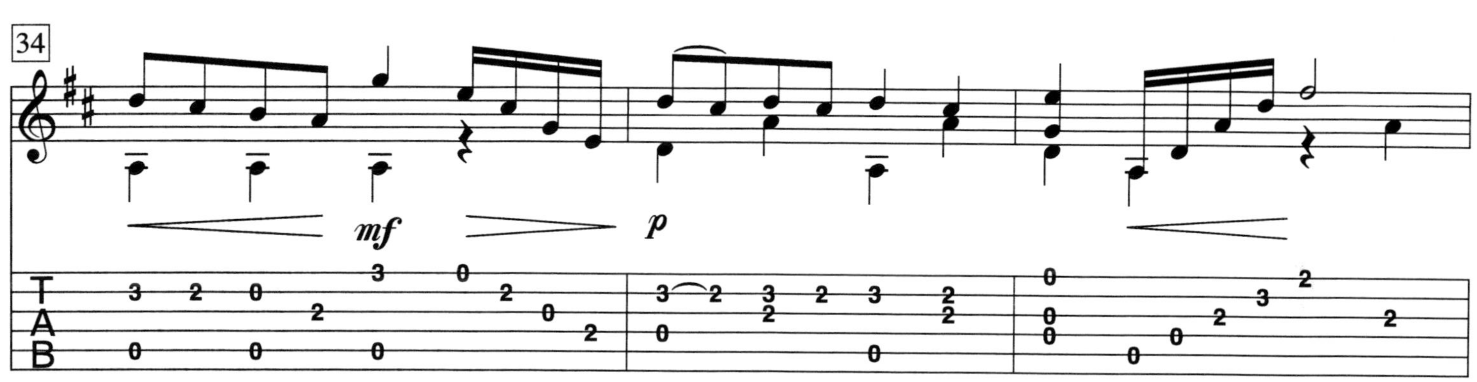
34
mf
p

37
mf
p

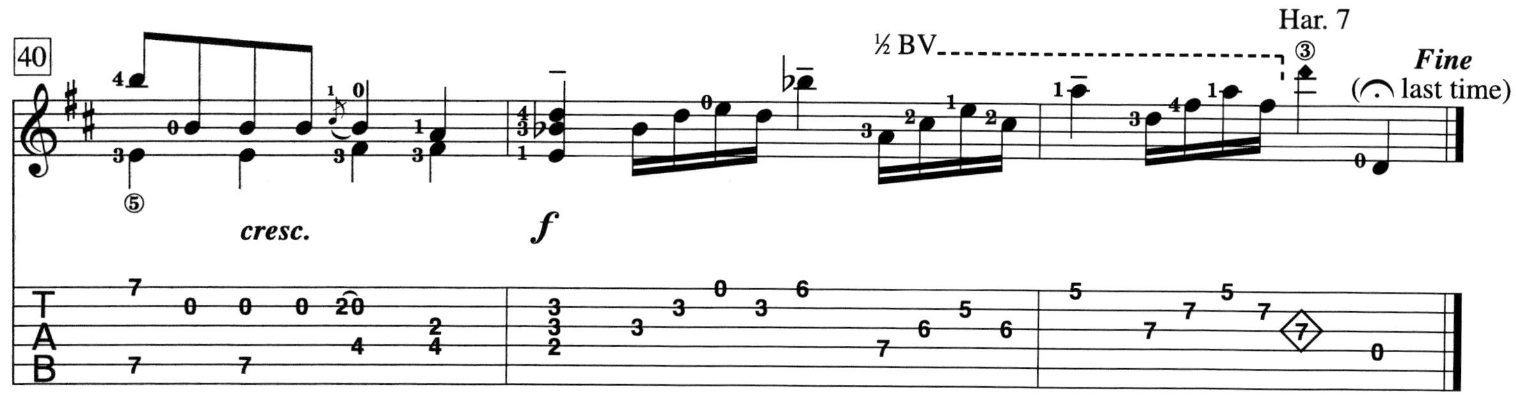
40
cresc.
f
½ BV
Har. 7
Fine
(last time)

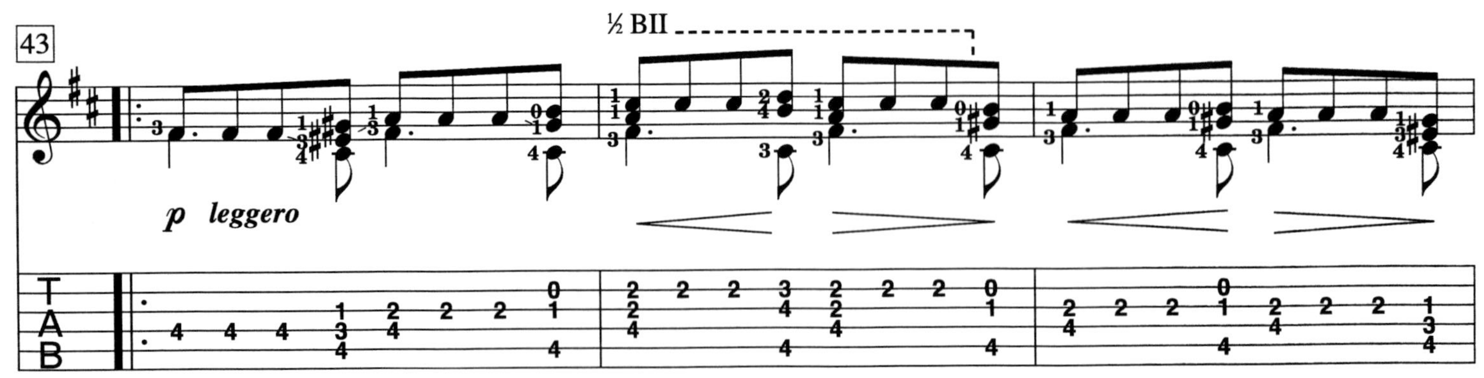
43
½ BII
p leggero

46
½ BII

49
1.
2.

D.S. al Fine
52

Waltz of the Flowers

*Original key D major

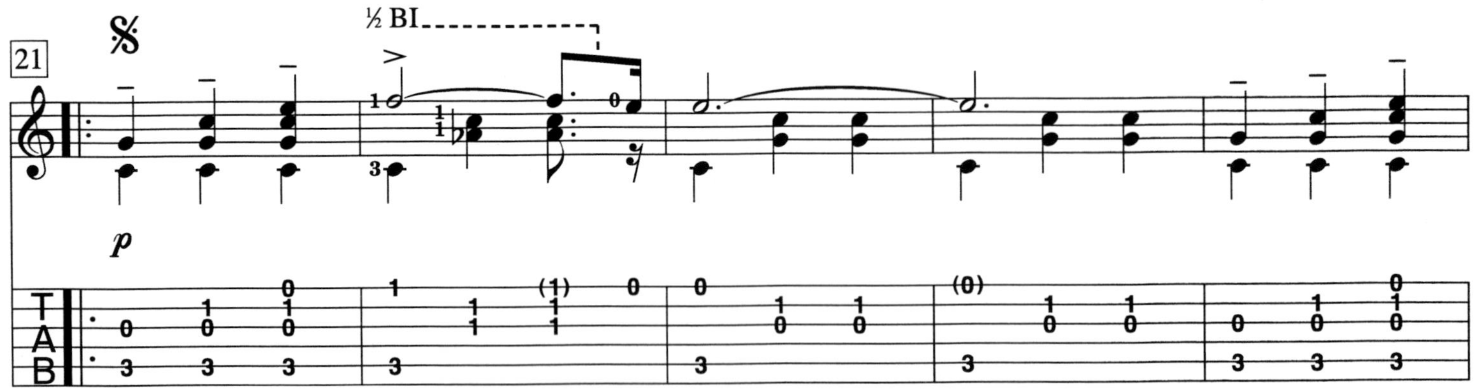
21
½ BI
p

26
½ BI
f
p

30
½ BI
Pos. III
Pos. IV
cresc.
mf

34
Pos. VII
p

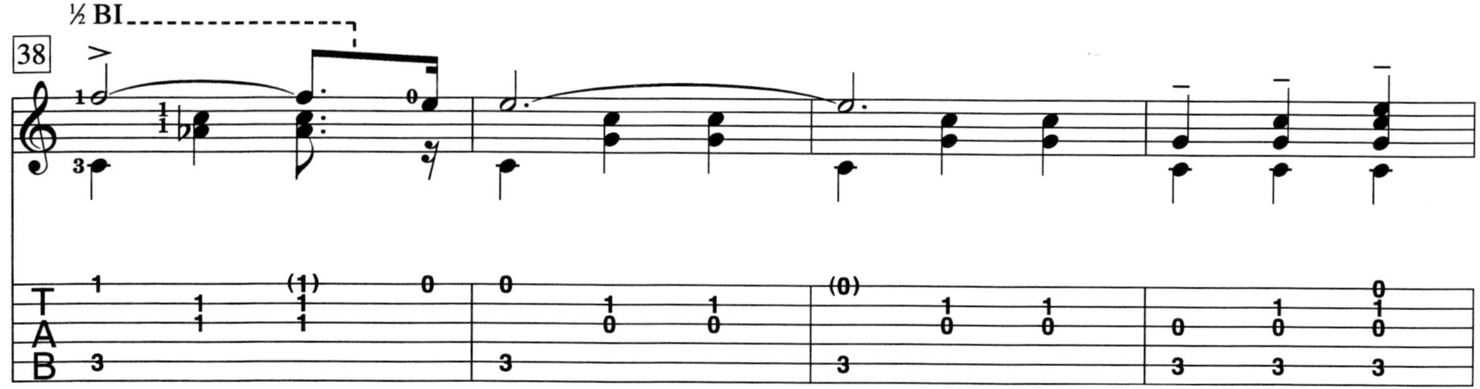
½ BI
38

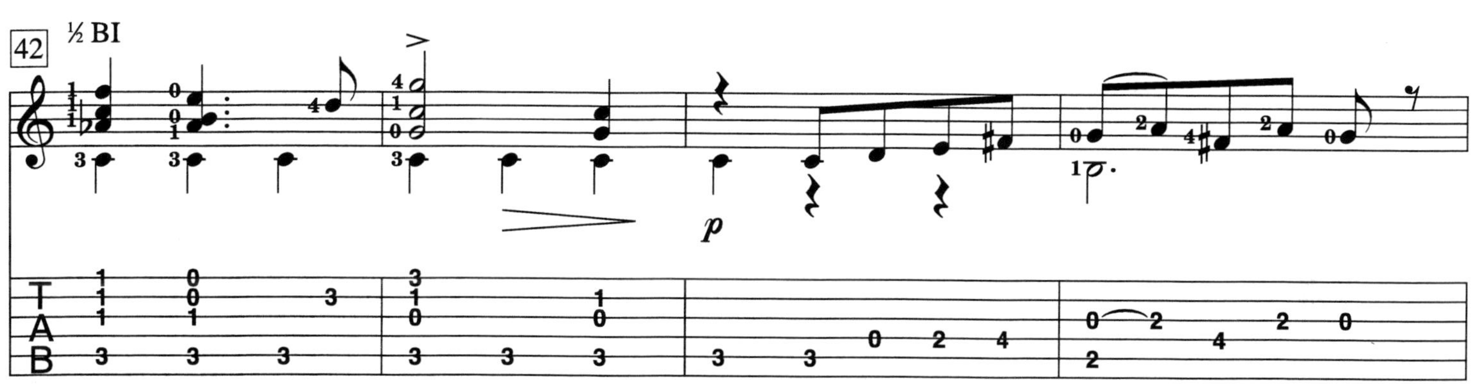
½ BI
42
p

46
mf

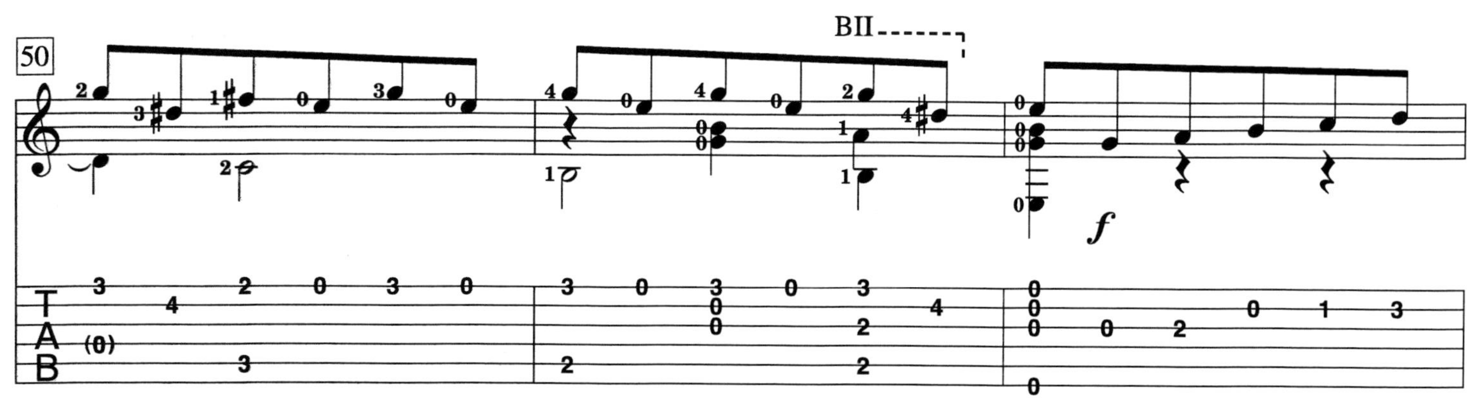
50
BII
f

53
dolce

½ BI
57

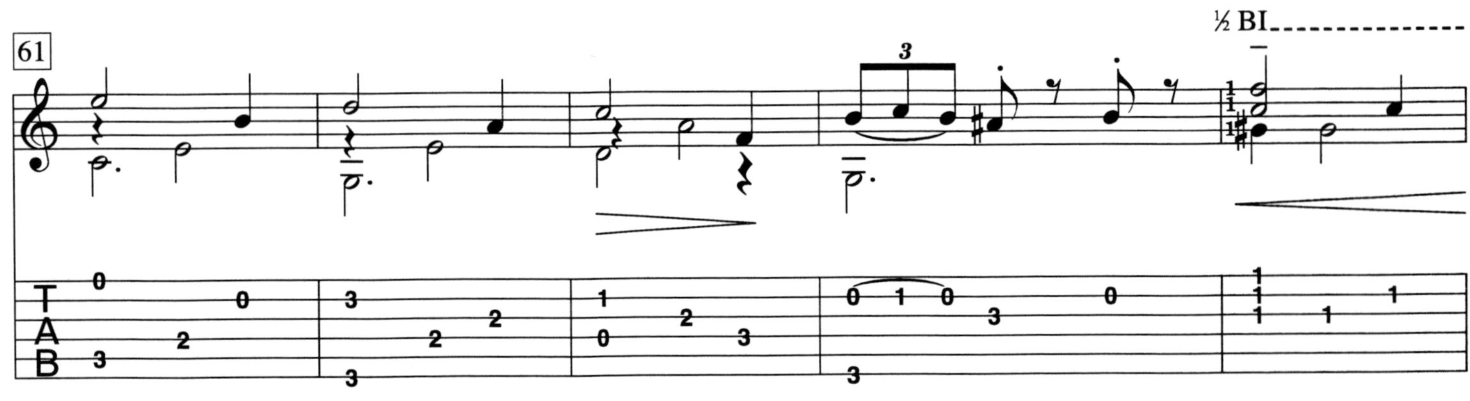
61
½ BI

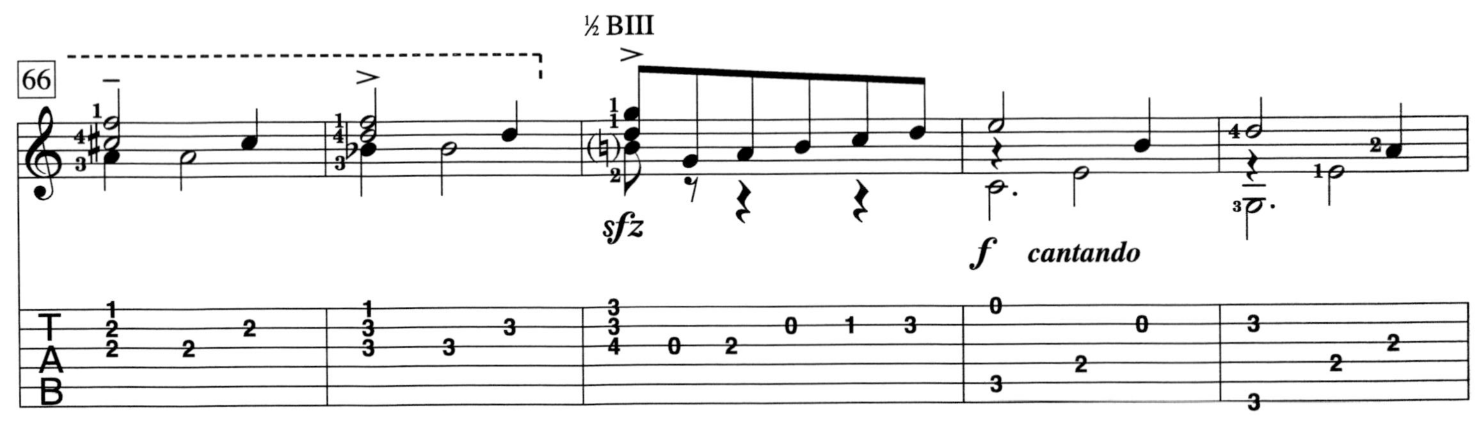
66
½ BIII
sfz
f cantando

71
½ BI

76
to Coda
f

81
1.
2.
sfz
sfz

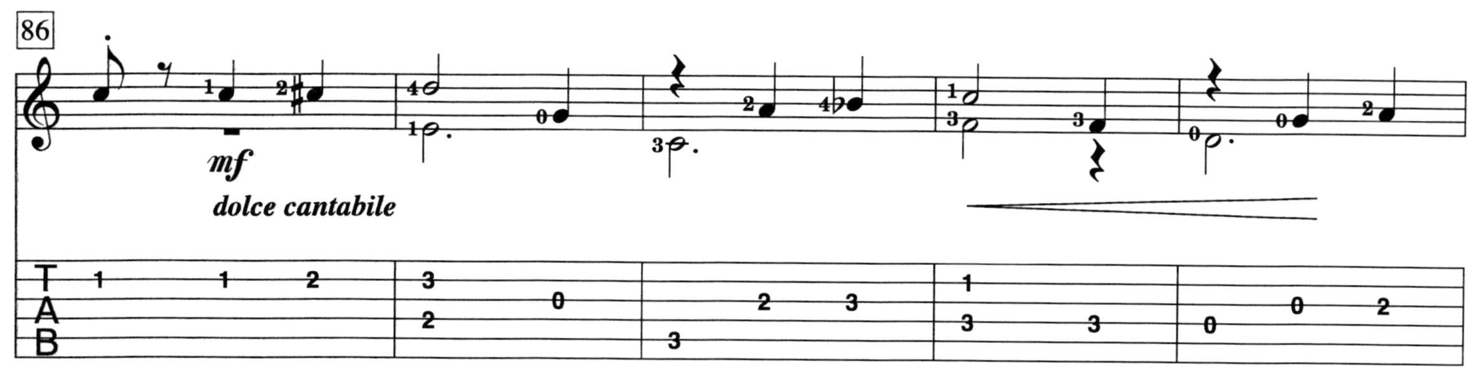
86
mf
dolce cantabile

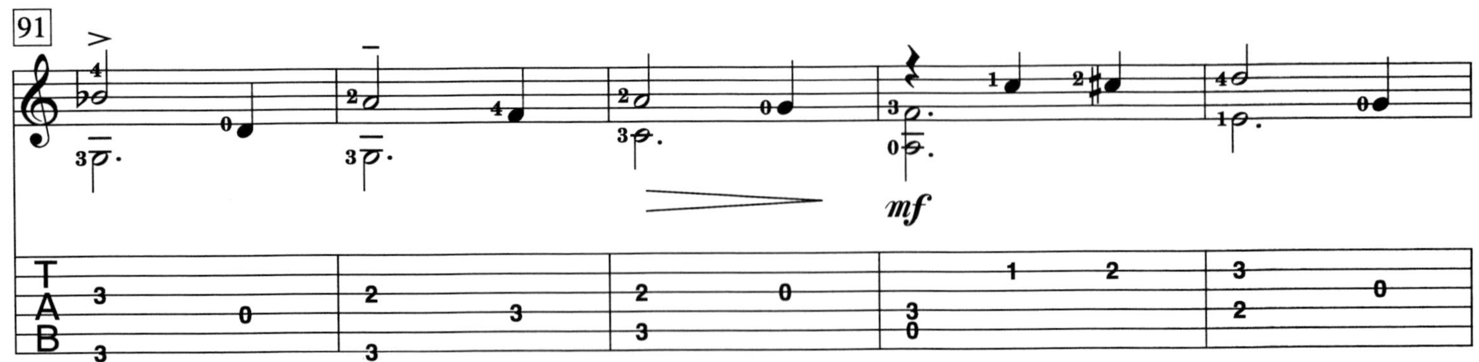
91
mf
T
A
B

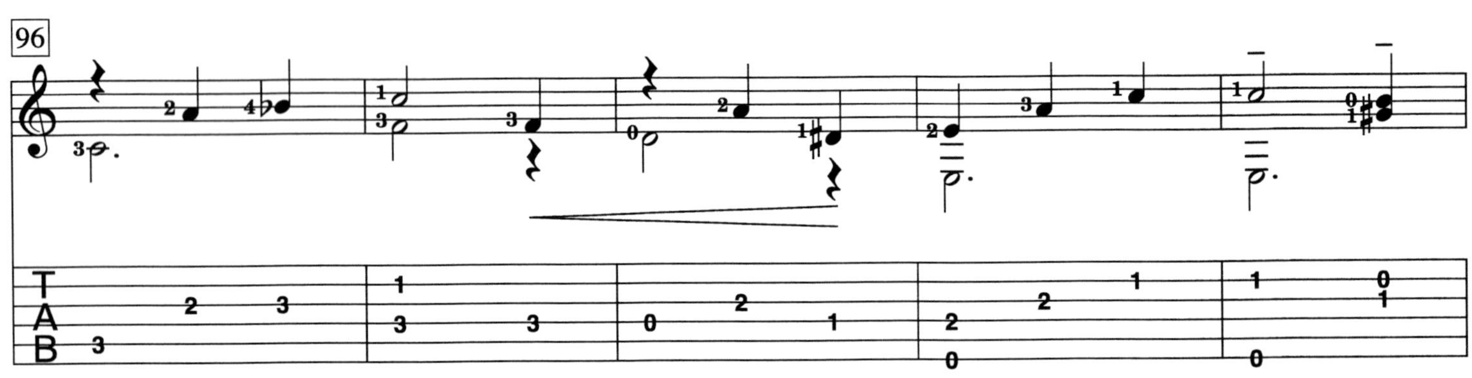
96
T
A
B

101
f
p dolce cantando
T
A
B

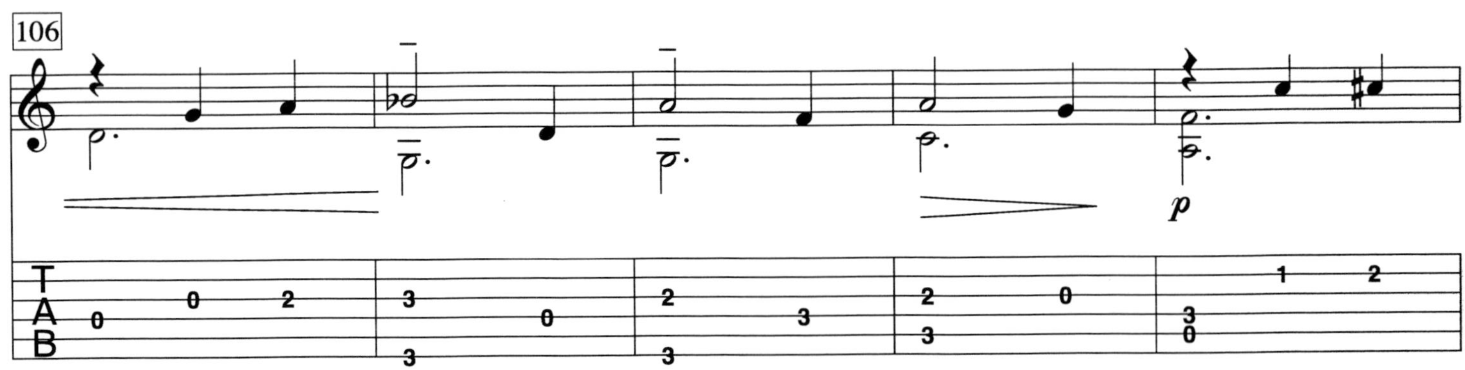
106
p
T
A
B

111
TAB

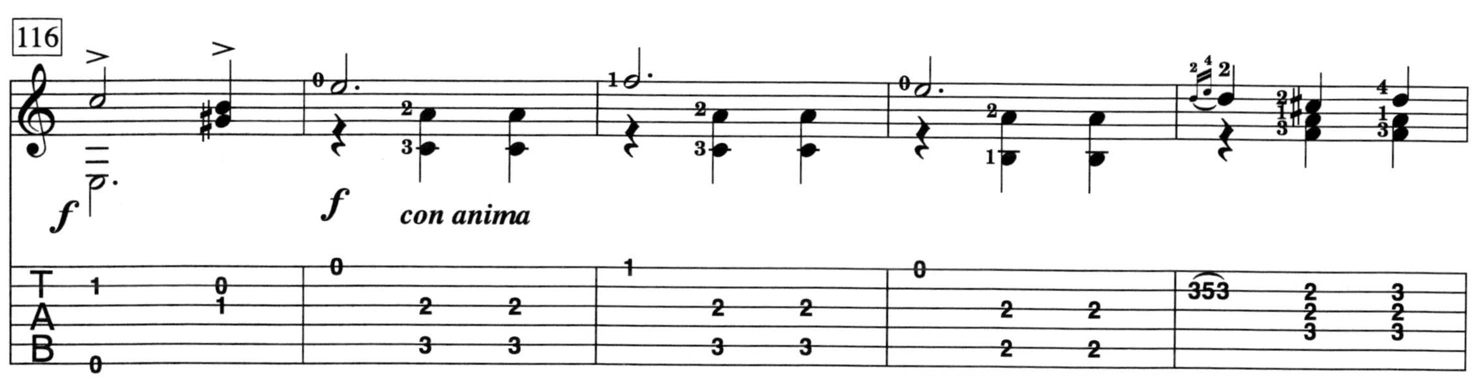
116
f
f
con anima
TAB

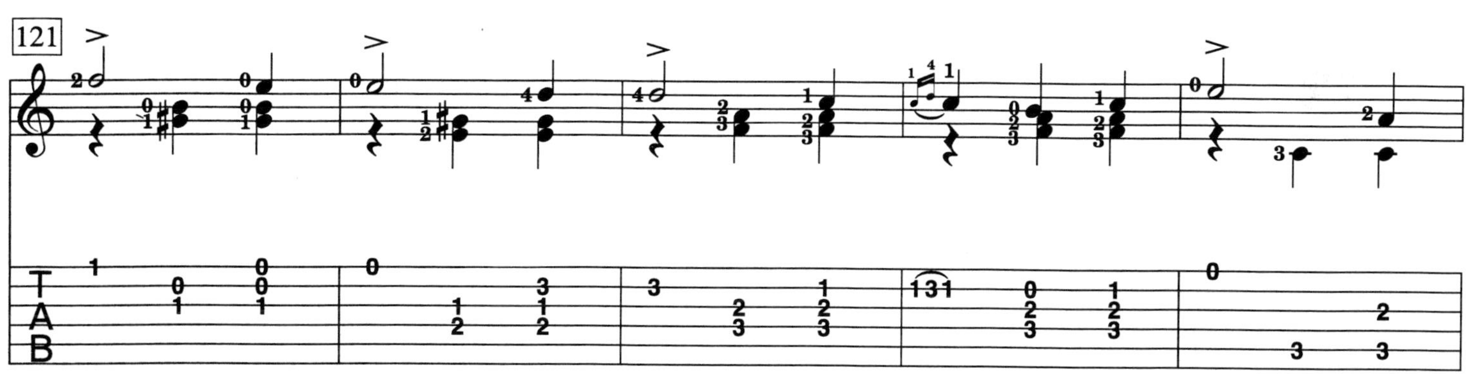
121
TAB

126
Pos. III
TAB

131
T
A
B

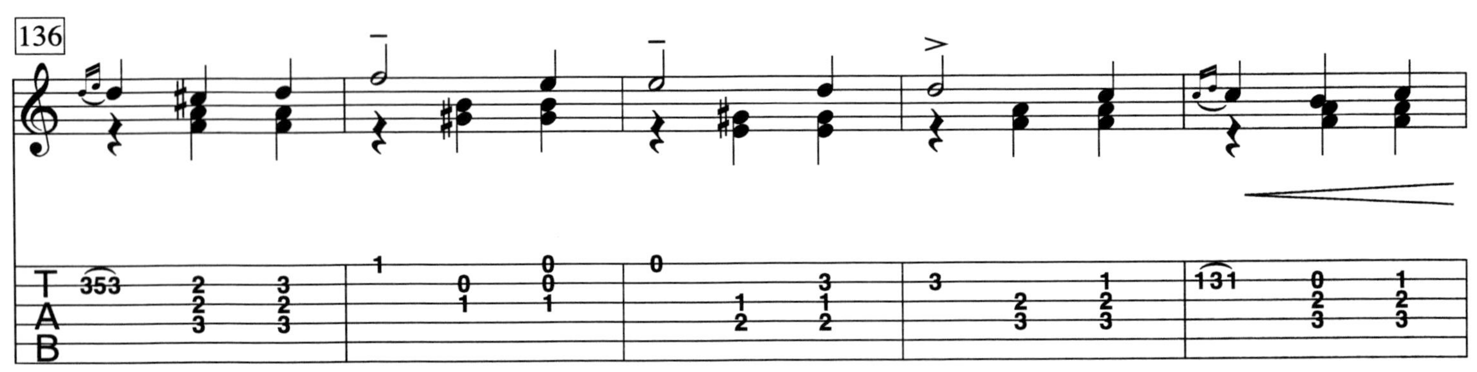
136
T
A
B

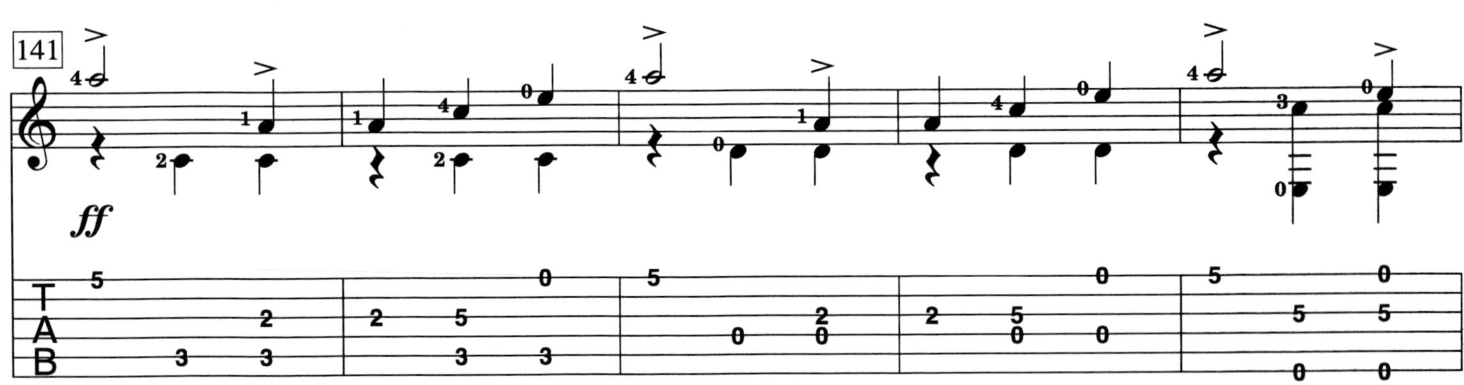
141
ff
T
A
B

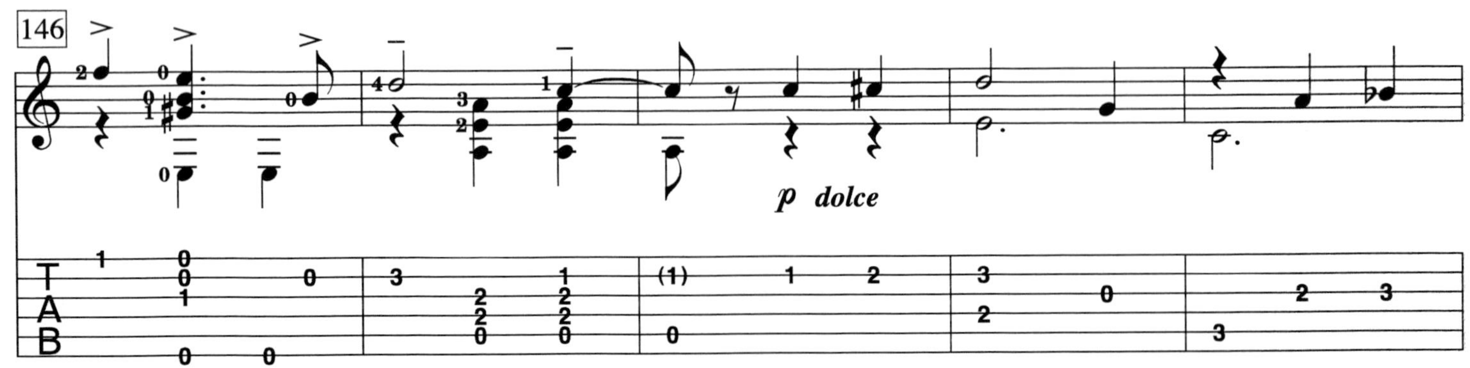
146
p dolce
T
A
B

151
156
⅔ BI
mp
161
cresc.
f
piu f
166
D.S. al Coda
ff
pp
Coda
Pos. V
Pos. VII